STUDY GUIDE

Douglas Hindman
Eastern Kentucky University

Abnormal Psychology

Eighth Edition

Gerald C. Davison
University of Southern California

John M. Neale
State University of New York at Stony Brook

JOHN WILEY & SONS, INC.
NEW YORK • CHICHESTER • WEINHEIM • BRISBANE • SINGAPORE • TORONTO

Cover Credit: "Camas Andinas" 1979 by Nemesio Antunez.
Kactus Foto, Santiago, Chile/Kactus Foto/Superstock

To order books or for customer service call 1-800-CALL-WILEY (225-5945).

ISBN 0-471-38699-5

Printed in the United States of America

10 9 8 7 6 5 4

Printed and bound by Courier Stoughton, Inc.

To My Students

This Study Guide is designed to help you study *Abnormal Psychology, 8th Edition* by Davison & Neale. Each chapter in this guide provides a variety of aids to make your study easier and more effective.

Overview sections place the chapter in context by describing its relationship to the chapters that precede and follow it.

Chapter Summary sections, not surprisingly, summarize the chapter.

Study Objectives list the important ideas or concepts to be learned in the chapter.

Key Terms provide a place for you to write in definitions of technical words introduced in the chapter. Typically, these terms are boldfaced in the text.

Study Questions are questions for you to answer as you read each section of the text. The Study Guide provides space for you to write your answers to each question. Research indicates that actually writing the answers is an effective way to study.

Self-Test provides a way for you to check your knowledge of the chapter. The Self-Test questions cover the content specified by the Study Questions, except for an occasional asterisked (*) test question.

The Study Guide begins with a chapter on *Studying in This Course (and in Other Courses Too).* This chapter is based on my experiences helping students improve their study skills. It describes a study method (SQ4R) you can use to improve your study skills. It also provides suggestions for coping with common study problems. I hope you'll find this chapter helpful.

Abnormal psychology is a fascinating, but complex, topic for many students. Hopefully, this Study Guide will make your study easier and more effective. It is based on the experiences, comments, and criticisms of hundreds of students who have used it in my classes. I invite you to join them in offering suggestions for further improvements.

Douglas Hindman
Berea, Kentucky

CONTENTS

Introduction

Studying in This Course (and in Other Courses Too)

I'm convinced, though it might be hard to prove, that few students get bad grades because they're dumb. There is little in the average college curriculum (including abnormal psychology) that's beyond the intellectual capacities of most college students. I'm convinced most students get poor grades because they don't know how to study.

Being a student is a job. The hours are long and the pay is nonexistent but it's still a job. The payoff is the knowledge you gain and the grades you get. You've been at this "job" for many years, and you're probably not through with it. If this is to be your job you might consider how to become really good at it. Are you learning? Are you working efficiently and getting the results you should?

This Study Guide incorporates features to help you develop good study skills. If you will spend a little time consciously working on your study skills, you can help the process along.

This chapter is intended to help you review and improve your study skills. The first part of the chapter describes a system, SQ4R, which you can use in this, or almost any, course. The second part of the chapter contains suggestions for dealing with common study problems.

◆ THE SQ4R STUDY SYSTEM

As you begin to study a new chapter, follow this plan.

SURVEY

First, survey the entire chapter briefly. Spend a few minutes getting a general idea of the material. Look over the titles, pictures, introduction, and summary in the text. Read the overview, chapter summary, and essential concepts in this Study Guide. While doing so, ask yourself what you will be studying. Figure out how the text is organized to cover the topic. Don't read the chapter in detail yet. This brief survey will help you focus your attention and become familiar with new vocabulary and concepts. Research suggests that initially surveying the chapter can reduce your overall study time by 40%.

QUESTION

Take the first portion of the chapter and ask yourself what you are about to study. The study questions in this Study Guide will help you formulate this question. In other courses, take the main heading or topic and turn it into a question.

READ

Then, read the first portion of the text looking for the answer to your question. It is important that you actively seek the answer as you read. Deliberately try *not* to read every word. Instead, read for answers.

Typically a text will make several points regarding each general topic. Look for words indicating these points such as, "first," "furthermore," or "finally." Generally a paragraph contains one idea. Additional paragraphs may elaborate on or illustrate the point. You may find it helpful to number each point in the text as you find it.

WRITE

Write down the answer in the space below the study question in your guide. In other courses, take study notes. This step is critical. By writing the answer you confirm that you actually understand it. Occasionally, when you try to write down your answer, you'll discover you don't understand the idea well enough to put it into words. That's okay. Go back and read some more until you figure it out.

As you write the answer, strive to use as few words as possible. Being concise is important. Try to come up with a few key words that convey the idea. When you can condense a long portion of text into a few key words that express the whole idea, you know you understand the idea clearly. The few key words you write down will be meaningful to you so you will remember them. Do not write complete sentences or elaborate excessively. The fewer words you can use, the better you probably understand and will remember the concept.

When you finish, go on to the next study question. Read, write, and repeat until you finish.

RECITE

After you finish the chapter, go back and quiz yourself. Do this aloud. Actively speaking and listening to yourself will help you remember. Look at each question and try to repeat the answer without looking. Cover your answers with a sheet of paper so you don't peek accidentally. If you've done the earlier steps well, this won't take much time.

REVIEW

Set aside a few minutes every week to recite the material again. Put several questions together and try to recite all the answers to a whole general topic. Do this regularly and you'll find it takes little time to refresh yourself for an exam.

Get with a classmate to quiz each other, or ask a friend to read the questions and tell you if your answers make sense. This step helps you understand (not just memorize) the material. As you discuss answers with someone else, you develop new ways of looking at the material. This can be especially helpful when the test questions aren't phrased quite the way you expected.

The technique above is one variation of a study method called "SQ4R" (Survey, Question, Read, Write, Recite, Review). If you're not used to it, it may seem a bit complicated at first. If you check around, though, you will find that the "good" students are already using it or a similar system. Research suggests that SQ4R works. It takes a bit of extra effort to get used to, but remember that studying is a skill and that learning any skill (like typing, driving, and playing ball) takes time and practice. You will find, though, that your efforts will pay off in this and in your other courses.

◆ COPING WITH STUDY PROBLEMS

The previous section of this chapter described an active study technique that has proven useful to many students. This section talks about common study complaints and what to do about them.

FINDING THE TIME

Does it seem like you never have time to study — or that you study all the time and still aren't getting results? Admittedly, study takes time, but let's look at the matter.

The traditional rule of thumb is that you should study two hours outside class for every hour in class. If that sounds like a lot, consider this. The average college student class load is 15 semester hours. If you study two hours for each class hour that's 30 additional hours for a "work week" of 45 hours.

If you have trouble finding that 45 hours, it's time to look at how you spend your time. Make a "time log." You can copy the time log at the end of this chapter or make one of your own. Use it to record how you spend your time for a week or so. Don't try to change what you're doing. Just record it.

After a week or so, stop and look at how you're using your time. There are 90 hours between 8 A.M. and 11 P.M. in a six-day week. If you devote half those hours to the "job" of being a student, you'll have 45 hours left. It's your time.

You may want to schedule your time differently. You'll need to decide what works for your style and situation. If you set up a schedule, be sure to include time for things you really enjoy as well as time to eat, do your laundry, etc.

Schedule adequate study time and actually spend it studying. If you get everything done and have time left over, use it to get ahead in one of your classes. When your study time is over, you should be able to enjoy other activities without worrying about your "job."

GETTING STARTED

Do you find it difficult to actually get down to work when it's study time? Many students find it helpful to find or make a specific study place. It could be a desk in your room, the library, or any place where you won't be disturbed and have access to your books and materials.

Use your study place *only* to study. If it *has* to be a place where you do other things, change it in some way when you use it to study. For example, if you use the kitchen table, clear it off and place a study light on it before you start to study. If you're interrupted, leave your study place until the interruption is over and you can return to studying.

If you do this, you'll soon get into the habit of doing nothing but studying in your study place and will be able to get to work as soon as you sit down.

READING THE MATERIAL

Some students believe that effective study means to "read the chapter" three or four times. This could be called the "osmosis approach" to studying. You expose yourself to the words in the text and hope something will sink in — like getting a sun tan. This approach does *not* work.

If you just "read the chapter" you'll often realize you've been looking at words but have no idea what they mean. If you come to a difficult idea, you're likely to skip over it. When you reread the chapter, you're likely to recall that the idea was difficult and skip over it again. The result is that you end up having read the chapter three or four times without understanding most of it.

Instead, use an active study technique like the SQ4R system described earlier. Research indicates that active study techniques can dramatically increase how quickly you learn material and how much of it you recall.

UNDERLINING THE TEXT

Many students underline (or highlight) their texts. Underlining works well — sometimes. For most people, underlining is not as efficient as taking notes. The danger in underlining is that you tend to underline things to be learned later rather than learning them now. Thus, you can end up with half the chapter underlined and none of it learned. If you *must* underline, try to underline as few words as possible in the same way as the "key words" approach described in the "Write" section earlier. Avoid used textbooks that someone else underlined. They may have been a poor underliner. More importantly, the value of underlining (like the value of taking notes) is in doing it yourself and in learning what's important in the process.

READING SPEED

Slow reading can lead to a number of problems. Most obviously, it takes too long to get through the material. More importantly, you lose interest before you get to the main point. You forget the first part of an idea before you get to the end. (You "lose the forest for the trees.") You may not understand a concept unless it's clearly stated in one sentence. You may misinterpret material because you take so long getting through it that you start reading in your own ideas.

If this description sounds familiar, you might want to check your reading speed. To check your speed, time yourself while you read for exactly five minutes. Estimate the total words you've read and divide by five. To estimate the total words you read, count the number of words in five lines and divide by five to get the average number of words per line. Then count the number of lines you read and multiply by the number of words per line.

For textbook material, an efficient reading speed is about 350 to 400 words per minute — depending on the difficulty of the topic and your familiarity with it. For novels and other leisure reading, many students can read 600 to 800 words per minute and "speed readers" can read much faster. Remember that understanding and flexibility in your reading style is more important than mere speed. But, often, increased speed actually improves your understanding.

You can increase your reading speed to some extent by conscious effort. If you watch someone read, you'll notice that their eyes move in "jerks" across the line. Our eyes can read words only when stopped. We read a group of words, move our eyes, read the next group, and so on. To increase reading speed, try to take in more words with each eye stop. Don't be concerned with every "and" or "but." Try to notice only words that carry meaning. Read for ideas, not words.

If you read very slowly, you should consider seeking special help. Most campuses have reading laboratories where you can get instruction in increasing your reading speed. Ask your instructor or advisor if your school offers such help.

ANALYZING TESTS

Perhaps you studied hard but still did poorly on the test. How can you make sure the same thing doesn't happen again?

You'll find it helpful to analyze what went wrong on each question you missed. You may be able to do this in class or you may need to see your instructor individually.

Compare the test and your study notes or Study Guide answers. Examine each question you got wrong and reconstruct what happened. For example, did you have the answer in your notes? If so, why didn't you recognize it on the test? Do this for each question you got wrong and look for a pattern. Here are some possibilities.

Was the answer not in your study notes at all? Perhaps you didn't answer all of a study question or, otherwise, missed important concepts. Perhaps you should talk to your instructor about his or her orientation to the course. What concepts or areas does he or she consider important? What does the instructor want you to learn? Ask the instructor to review your notes and point out where you omitted things he or she considers important.

If your study notes seem complete, go back and compare them to the text. Perhaps you misread the text, got the concept wrong, or only got part of it. Make sure you read the entire section of the text. Sometimes the first sentence of a paragraph only *seems* to convey the idea. Later sentences (or paragraphs) may really convey the core idea. Perhaps, also, you need to read faster. Slow readers often have trouble with complex concepts that aren't clearly stated in one sentence.

Perhaps the answer was in your study notes but you didn't remember it on the test. You can be pleased that you had it in your notes — but why didn't you remember it? Were you too tense? Do you need to recite and review more?

Perhaps you knew the answer but didn't recognize it because of the way the question was phrased. That suggests you're stressing memorization too much. Try to review with someone else. Get them to make you explain your answers and discuss ways they would say it differently. This will help you understand ideas when they are stated differently.

MORE HELP

Many schools have a learning lab or learning skills center where you can get individualized help. Ask your instructor what facilities your school provides.

For ideas on using this time log, see "Finding the Time," page ix.

Time Log

Date ________________________

Time	Doing what?	Where?	Comments
7:00 -	-	-	
7:30 -	-	-	
8:00 -	-	-	
8:30 -	-	-	
9:00 -	-	-	
9:30 -	-	-	
10:00 -	-	-	
10:30 -	-	-	
11:00 -	-	-	
11:30 -	-	-	
12:00 -	-	-	
12:30 -	-	-	
1:00 -	-	-	
1:30 -	-	-	
2:00 -	-	-	
2:30 -	-	-	
3:00 -	-	-	
3:30 -	-	-	
4:00 -	-	-	
4:30 -	-	-	
5:00 -	-	-	
5:30 -	-	-	
6:00 -	-	-	
6:30 -	-	-	
7:00 -	-	-	
7:30 -	-	-	
8:00 -	-	-	
8:30 -	-	-	
9:00 -	-	-	
9:30 -	-	-	
10:00 -	-	-	
10:30 -	-	-	
11:00 -	-	-	
11:30 -	-	-	
12:00 -	-	-	

Chapter 1

Introduction: Historical and Scientific Considerations

◆ OVERVIEW

The first five chapters cover basic ideas and issues in abnormal psychology. These chapters are the background for the rest of the text, which covers the various forms of psychopathology and related topics.

The first two chapters discuss viewpoints on the nature of psychopathology. For example, should people with psychological problems be viewed as "sick," as having "adjustment problems," or as the victims of faulty socialization or learning?

The way we view these problems becomes especially important when discussing ways of classifying and studying psychopathology, which are covered in Chapters 3, 4, and 5. For example, if we view people with these problems as being "mentally ill," then we would want to focus on the illness, developing ways to study, diagnose, and treat it. If, instead, we perceive these people as having learned ineffective behaviors, then we will want to categorize and treat their behavior differently.

CHAPTER SUMMARY

Chapter 1 covers three major topics.

What Is Abnormal Behavior? offers five characteristics of abnormality. None are, by themselves, adequate definitions of abnormality but, together, they provide a framework for understanding it.

The *History of Psychopathology* shows that different historical periods have emphasized one of three views concerning the causes of psychopathology: demonology (caused by evil outside forces), somatogenesis (bodily causes), or psychogenesis (psychological or mental causes). These three views have led society to view and treat disturbed individuals in very different ways.

Science: A Human Enterprise points out that science is never totally objective. It is influenced by the human beings who conduct it. Scientific research questions and data are influenced by the incomplete knowledge of scientists and by their views or assumptions about reality. These assumptions or paradigms influence the kinds of data scientists seek and the way they make sense out of what they find. Paradigms can also make it difficult for scientists to recognize phenomena that don't fit their paradigm.

ESSENTIAL CONCEPTS

1. Abnormality can be characterized in various ways. None of the characteristics hold up perfectly but, together, they provide a framework for understanding abnormality.

2. Throughout history there have been differing views on the cause of abnormal behavior. Generally abnormal behavior has been attributed to outside forces (demonology), bodily factors (somatogenesis), or mental factors (psychogenesis).

3. Contemporary views are based largely on the somatogenic and the psychogenic viewpoints.

4. The way different societies understand abnormal behavior strongly affects the way they treat it.

5. Past methods of treating abnormal behavior have varied and, often, been inhuman. However, they may not have been as bad as portrayed nor are current practices as enlightened as sometimes depicted.

6. Although science strives to be objective, it is influenced by the limited knowledge and the subjective views of scientists.

7. Paradigms or subjective assumptions are inevitable in any science. They influence what data scientists seek and what questions they ask.

KEY TERMS

Psychopathology (p. 3)

Abnormal behavior (p. 3)

Normal [or bell-shaped] curve (p. 4)

Clinicians (p. 6)

Clinical psychologist (p. 6)

Diagnosis (p. 6)

Psychotherapy (p. 6)

Psychiatrist (p. 6)

Psychoactive drugs (p. 6)

TO MY STUDENTS

Before you plunge into this study guide, you might take a few minutes to understand it. After all, a study guide is a tool — and tools are most useful if you learn to use them properly.

This study guide comes out of my experience with what helps my students in abnormal psychology. It is designed to help them, and you, learn the material more effectively and efficiently.

The introductory chapter in this guide (entitled *Studying in This Course*) describes how to study effectively and provides suggestions for common study problems. Studying is a skill that can be learned. Read the introductory chapter for ideas on how to improve your own study skills.

For each chapter of the text, begin by reading the *Overview, Chapter Summary,* and *Essential Concepts* sections in this guide. These sections provide a broad outline of the chapter and how it fits into the overall text. That information will improve your studying later by helping you see how various details are part of broader topics.

The *Key Terms* section lists new technical terms introduced in the chapter. There is space for you to write in definitions, which is an excellent way for you to learn and study these terms.

The *Study Questions* provide you a guide for studying the chapter by identifying the important ideas in each part. Read the first question, then study the indicated pages looking for the answer. Write notes on the answers you find in the space provided. Review these notes later for tests.

The *Self-Test* provides multiple-choice and short-answer questions you can use to test your knowledge.

Finally the *Visual Summary* provides a graphic review of the chapter's key concepts and their relationships.

I hope you will enjoy and benefit from your study of abnormal psychology and from this study guide. I welcome your comments, criticisms, and suggestions. Please feel free to write me at the address on the title page.

Psychoanalyst (p. 6)

Psychiatric social worker (p. 6)

Counseling psychologist (p. 6)

Psychopathologist (p. 6)

Demonology (p. 7)

Exorcism (p. 7)

Somatogenesis (p. 7)

Psychogenesis (p. 7)

Asylums (p. 9)

Moral treatment (p. 11)

Syndrome (p. 12)

General Paresis (p. 13)

Germ theory [of disease] (p. 13)

Milieu Therapy (p. 14)

Cathartic method (p. 16)

Paradigm (p. 17)

◆ STUDY QUESTIONS

WHAT IS ABNORMAL BEHAVIOR? (p. 3–7)

1. Briefly describe five characteristics of abnormality. Explain the strengths and weaknesses of each in defining abnormality. Explain how these characteristics, collectively, form a framework for understanding abnormality. (p. 3–7)

HISTORY OF PSYCHOPATHOLOGY (p. 7–16)

2. Describe demonology and somatogenesis as early theories of the causes of deviant behavior. How did each explain abnormality? What kinds of treatment resulted from these explanations? (p. 7–8)

3. According to many historians, how did views and treatment of mental illness change during the Dark Ages and change again starting in the thirteenth century? What evidence suggests that the mentally ill were considered witches — and what evidence suggests they were not? (p. 8–9)

4. Describe the development of asylums for the mentally ill during the fifteenth and sixteenth centuries. How were the mentally ill treated in these early asylums? (p. 9–10)

5. Describe the development of moral treatment under Pinel and others. How did this approach view and treat mental illness? Why was this approach largely abandoned? (p. 10–12)

6. Describe the development of contemporary views of somatogenesis and psychogenesis. Include the contributions of Kraepelin, Pasteur, Mesmer, Charcot, and Breuer. (p. 12–16)

SCIENCE: A HUMAN ENTERPRISE (p. 16–18)

7. Identify an advantage and a disadvantage of the fact that science is conducted by human beings. (p. 16–17)

8. Science is also limited by the subjectivity of scientists. Explain this by defining paradigms and their role in science. Why are paradigms (a) necessary and (b) potentially limiting for scientists? (p. 17)

9. Describe the work of Langer and Abelson (1974) as an example of paradigms in abnormal psychology. How does their study illustrate the role of paradigms? (p. 17–18)

◆ SELF-TEST, CHAPTER 1

(* Items not covered in Study Questions.)

MULTIPLE-CHOICE

1. An illustration of abnormal behavior would be
   a. soiling oneself once a month at age 14.
   b. experiencing anxiety when engaged in rituals while leaving the house.
   c. losing control of oneself in anger, with no apparent provocation.
   d. All of the above are examples of abnormal behavior.

2. Which of the following illustrates a difficulty in defining abnormal behavior as behavior that is statistically infrequent?
   a. IQ below 70 is considered mentally retarded.
   b. It is unusual for people to have delusions.
   c. Math prodigies are rare in the population.
   d. Bedwetting is common in young children.

*3. Only psychiatrists can
   a. diagnose mental illness.
   b. conduct research.
   c. conduct psychotherapy.
   d. prescribe medication.

4. Demonology was the
   a. practice of exorcism
   b. devil worship and satanic cults that some viewed as causing mental illness
   c. idea that an evil being may live in a person and control his or her mind and body
   d. somatogenic hypothesis of mental illness

5. The "Malleus Maleficarum" was
   a. a witch hunt manual
   b. a ceremonial guide used by witches
   c. a treatment manual used in early mental hospitals
   d. a Freudian perspective on mental illness

6. Treatment for the mentally ill became more humane when
   a. moral treatment was introduced
   b. asylums were abolished
   c. abnormal behavior was seen as based upon medical problems
   d. specialty hospital wards were created for the mentally ill within general care facilities

7. The early classification system developed by Kraepelin
   a. was based on the psychogenic hypothesis
   b. was not influential in later diagnostic manuals
   c. emphasized the continuity of mental illness from normal to abnormal
   d. assumed each disorder was a distinct entity

8. When a group of symptoms typically co-occur, they are called
   a. syndromes
   b. mental disorders
   c. diagnoses
   d. clusters

9. Ivy experienced paralysis in her left arm, but there was no neurological basis for her symptoms. This is an illustration of
   a. psychogenic fugue
   b. hysteria
   c. posttraumatic stress disorder
   d. panic disorder

10. Dr. Jones is an adherent to the psychoanalytic paradigm. Dr. Smith prefers the behavioral paradigm. What will Dr. Smith feel about Dr. Jones' data collection procedures?
   a. that they are valid
   b. that they are objective
   c. that they are useless
   d. that they are false

SHORT ANSWER

1. What is a limitation of defining abnormality as violation of norms?

2. What kinds of treatments evolved from early demonology?

3. Hippocrates argued that deviant behavior was not punishment by the gods but a result of . .

4. What evidence suggests that most "witches" were *not* mentally ill?

5. How were the mentally ill treated in early asylums?

6. Why was moral treatment largely abandoned?

7. What is an advantage of the fact that science is conducted by human beings?

8. In what way is science (a) objective and (b) subjective?

9. Langer and Abelson's study illustrates the role of paradigms in psychology. Describe what they did.

10. In what way does Langer and Abelson's research illustrate the role of paradigms?

◆ ANSWERS TO SELF-TEST, CHAPTER 1

MULTIPLE-CHOICE

1. d (p. 4–5)	2. c (p. 4)	3. d (p. 6)	4. c (p. 7)
5. a (p. 8)	6. a (p. 10)	7. d (p. 12–13)	8. a (p. 12–13)
9. b (p. 13–15)	10. c (p. 17)		

SHORT ANSWER

1. People with some problems (like anxiety) do not appear different. Also norms vary across cultures. (p. 4)

2. Attempts to induce the demons to leave through prayer, drive them out through torture, etc. (p. 7)

3. Natural causes. (p. 7)

4. Apparent "hallucinations" of witches were extracted under torture. Government and hospitals recognized and provided for mentally ill. (p. 9)

5. Confined with lepers and social outcasts under poor conditions. Some asylums sold tickets to people who found their behavior amusing. (p. 10)

6. Public hospitals became too large to provide individual care. Physicians gained control and shifted focus to biological factors. (p. 11)

7. Science can benefit from their human ingenuity, scholarship, creativity, understanding, etc. (p. 17)

8. Objective in the observation and collection of data. Subjective in that observations are organized based on subjective paradigms. (p. 17)

9. Behavioral and psychoanalytic therapists viewed a videotape of a man described as either a job applicant or a patient. Then they rated the man's mental health. (p. 17)

10. The two groups of clinicians saw the same tape but, because of their paradigms, reached different conclusions. (p. 18)

Chapter 2

Current Paradigms in Psychopathology and Therapy

◆ OVERVIEW

This is the second of five introductory chapters covering topics that are basic to the rest of the text. Chapter 1 discussed the role of paradigms in science generally and traced the paradigms that have been important in the history of psychopathology. Many of the differences underlying those paradigms are still unresolved. In particular, the relationship between physical and psychological factors in pathology is still widely debated. As the field has developed, other distinctions have also emerged. These distinctions underlie the current paradigms that are described in Chapter 2. These current paradigms will be used to help understand and study the various types of psychopathology described later in the text.

Chapters 3 and 4 will deal with the topics of classification and assessment. They describe the current categories of psychopathology and the methods used to assess individuals who may have psychological problems. There are a number of issues and controversies involved in both classifying pathology and assessing individuals. Not surprisingly these reflect differences among the various paradigms presented in Chapters 1 and 2.

Chapter 5 will discuss research methods in psychopathology. Then the text will begin covering the major forms of abnormality.

CHAPTER SUMMARY

Chapter 2 describes five current paradigms: the biological, psychoanalytic, humanistic/existential, learning, and cognitive paradigms. Each paradigm is a viewpoint or set of assumptions about how to understand, study, and treat psychopathology.

The Biological Paradigm assumes that psychopathology, like medical disease, results from organic factors. It has led to research into behavior genetics and brain biochemistry. Biological treatments may have little relation to knowledge about biological factors in the disorder. This paradigm can also lead to reductionistic distortions.

The Psychoanalytic Paradigm originated with Sigmund Freud who looked for psychological origins of psychopathology in repressed or unconscious processes originating in childhood conflicts. Psychoanalytic techniques help lift the repression so that, as adults, we can face and handle the conflicts. Neo-Freudian analysts have shifted the emphasis from Freud's drive-based views and developed briefer therapies. Although criticized, Freud's insights underlie many contemporary ideas in abnormal psychology.

Humanistic and Existential Paradigms also promote insight but focus on understanding each unique individual and on the choices each individual can and must make in life. Humanistic therapy assumes people will make good, growth-enhancing choices when they feel accepted and valued. Existential therapy stresses, more, the inherent anxiety of making choices and accepting their consequences. Gestalt therapy fosters awareness of the immediate here-and-now in which choices are, inevitably, made.

Learning Paradigms reject mentalistic approaches and view psychopathology as ineffective behavior acquired through principles of classical conditioning, operant conditioning, and modeling. Mediational approaches extend learning principles to internal processes such as anxiety. These approaches have led to more precise methods of studying pathology and to improved treatments.

The Cognitive Paradigm considers a more complex view of learning, emphasizing that individuals actively integrate and interpret new experiences in terms of their existing understandings. Psychopathology is viewed in terms of ineffective understandings or irrational beliefs that may be relearned. This paradigm has led to popular, effective treatment methods. Cognitive therapists share many beliefs and techniques with behavioral therapists.

The *Consequences of Adopting a Paradigm* are to both focus and limit the search for answers. *Diathesis-stress: An Integrative Paradigm* may help integrate various viewpoints by considering multiple physical and psychological predispositions (diatheses) to react abnormally to particular environmental stress. *Different Perspectives on a Clinical Problem* illustrates how the same problem can make sense from a variety of paradigms. *Eclecticism in Psychotherapy* is common as therapists adjust their treatments based on a variety of paradigms.

ESSENTIAL CONCEPTS

1. Currently five major paradigms (sets of assumptions) are popular ways of understanding psychopathology. Each paradigm has evolved characteristic terminology, research, and therapeutic approaches.

2. The biological paradigm assumes that the roots of psychopathology are somatic or bodily in nature. This paradigm has produced extensive research on behavior genetics and brain biochemistry. Psychoactive drugs are used to alter functioning; although their use may not be based on knowledge about causes of the problem. The paradigm risks making reductionistic assumptions that behavior should be understood in terms of more "basic" or "underlying" biological factors.

3. The psychoanalytic paradigm assumes that psychopathology results from unconscious or repressed conflicts. Several variations have developed based on Freud's ideas about the structure of the mind, psychosexual stages of development, anxiety, and defenses. Psychoanalysts seek to lift repression so people can deal directly with conflicts.

4. Humanistic and existential paradigms assume that people can develop and change as they feel valued and supported. These therapists attempt to provide conditions in which clients can make their own choices.

5. Learning paradigms assert that abnormal behavior is learned much as normal behavior is learned. Three major learning processes have emerged: classical conditioning, operant conditioning, and mediational learning. These same processes can be used to change behavior.

6. The cognitive paradigm views people as active learners who understand current experiences in relation to their existing cognitions. Ineffective cognitions can lead to pathology. The learning and cognitive paradigms often overlap in practice.

7. The diathesis-stress paradigm is an attempt to integrate these paradigms in accounting for abnormal behavior.

8. In practice, most therapists are eclectic, blending elements from various paradigms to individualize treatment.

TO MY STUDENTS

I urge you to pay particular attention to this chapter.

The paradigms in Chapter 2 are a framework for much of the rest of the text. Recall that any paradigm consists of assumptions leading to particular methods of research and theorizing. Thus each paradigm has its own methods, terminology, and approaches to treatment. The paradigms in Chapter 2 (including assumptions, methods, and terms) will be used in discussing the various forms of abnormality presented throughout the text. By getting a clear understanding of each paradigm now, you'll find it much easier to make sense of the more detailed discussions later.

In addition, these are present-day paradigms. Try to identify which of them best fits your own personal paradigm (assumptions) about abnormality. This will help you recognize and evaluate your own inclinations throughout the course.

KEY TERMS

Biological paradigm (p. 21)

Medical [disease] model (p. 21)

Genes (p. 21)

Behavior genetics (p. 21)

Genotype (p. 21)

Phenotype (p. 21)

Family method (p. 22)

Index cases [probands] (p. 22)

Twin method (p. 22)

Monozygotic [MZ] twins (p. 22)

Dizygotic [DZ] twins (p. 22)

Concordance (p. 22)

Linkage analysis (p. 23)

Neuron (p. 23)

Nerve impulse (p. 23)

Synapse (p. 23)

Neurotransmitters (p. 23)

Reuptake (p. 24)

Psychoanalytic [psychodynamic] paradigm (p. 25)

Id (p. 26)

Libido (p. 26)

Unconscious (p. 26)

Pleasure principle (p. 26)

Primary process (p. 26)

Ego (p. 26)

Secondary process (p. 26)

Reality principle (p. 26)

Superego (p. 26)

Psychodynamics (p. 26)

Psychosexual stages (p. 26)

Oral stage (p. 26–27)

Anal stage (p. 27)

Phallic stage (p. 27)

Latency period (p. 27)

Genital stage (p. 27)

Fixation (p. 27)

Oedipus complex (p. 27)

Electra complex (p. 27)

Objective [realistic] anxiety (p. 27)

Neurotic anxiety (p. 27)

Defense mechanism (p. 28)

Repression (p. 28)

Projection (p. 28)

Displacement (p. 28)

Reaction formation (p. 28)

Regression (p. 28)

Rationalization (p. 28)

Sublimation (p. 28)

Analytical psychology (p. 29)

Collective unconscious (p. 30)

Individual psychology (p. 30)

Psychotherapy (p. 31)

Insight therapies (p. 31)

Action therapies (p. 31)

Free association (p. 31)

Resistance (p. 31)

Dream analysis (p. 32)

Latent content (p. 32)

Transference (p. 32)

Countertransference (p. 32)

Interpretation (p. 32)

Ego analysts (p. 33)

Brief therapy (p. 33)

Interpersonal therapy (p. 34)

Humanistic and existential therapies (p. 35)

Unconditional positive regard (p. 36)

Gestalt therapy (p. 38)

Learning paradigm (p. 41)

Introspection (p. 41)

Behaviorism (p. 41)

Classical conditioning (p. 41)

Unconditioned stimulus [UCS] (p. 41)

Unconditioned response [UCR] (p. 41)

Conditioned stimulus [CS] (p. 41)

Conditioned response [CR] (p. 42)

Extinction (p. 42)

Law of effect (p. 42)

Instrumental learning (p. 42)

Operant conditioning (p. 42)

Discriminative stimulus (p. 42)

Positive reinforcement (p. 42)

Negative reinforcement (p. 43)

Shaping (p. 43)

Successive approximations (p. 43)

Modeling (p. 43)

Mediational theory of learning (p. 44)

Mediator (p. 44)

Avoidance conditioning (p. 44)

Behavior therapy (p.44)

Behavior modification (p. 44)

Counterconditioning (p. 45)

Systematic desensitization (p. 45)

Aversive conditioning (p. 46)

Time out (p. 46)

Token economy (p. 46)

Role playing (p. 48)

Behavior rehearsal (p. 48)

Cognition (p. 49)

Cognitive paradigm (p. 49)

Schema (p. 49)

Assertion training (p. 50)

Cognitive behavior therapy (p. 51)

Cognitive restructuring (p. 51)

Irrational beliefs (p. 51)

Rational-emotive behavior therapy (p. 51)

Self-efficacy (p. 53)

Diathesis-stress (p. 55)

◆ STUDY QUESTIONS

THE BIOLOGICAL PARADIGM (p. 21–25)

1. What are the assumptions of the biological paradigm? Describe the behavior genetics view of the relationship between genes and abnormal behavior. Describe four research methods in behavior genetics and any limitations of each. (p. 21–23)

2. Describe the biochemistry of the nervous system, especially neurotransmitters. Identify three neurotransmitter problems that could be linked to psychopathology. (p. 23–24)

3. Briefly describe three relationships between treatment and knowledge that a disorder has biological causes. Evaluate the biological paradigm by defining reductionism and the problem with it. (p. 24–25)

THE PSYCHOANALYTIC PARADIGM (p. 25–35)

4. What is the central assumption of the psychoanalytic paradigm? Briefly describe Freud's classical theory including, three mental functions, how they interact, and four (or five) stages of psychosexual development. (p. 25–27)

5. How does neurotic anxiety develop according to Freud's earlier and later theories? (Pay attention to what is repressed in each theory.) How do defense mechanisms minimize anxiety — and indicate it exists? How did Freud's changing views on childhood relationships influence his theory? (p. 27–29)

6. The text summarizes two Neo-Freudian theorists. In what way did they continue Freud's tradition? Describe about three new concepts developed by each theorist. (p. 29–30)

7. According to psychoanalytic therapy, what can happen once repression is lifted? Describe four techniques and how each helps in reaching the goal of lifting repression. (p. 30–32)

8. Identify three modifications of psychoanalytic therapy. Describe the major assumption of each and how therapy methods changed as a result. Evaluate the psychoanalytic paradigm by identifying four criticisms and four contributions. (p. 32–35)

HUMANISTIC AND EXISTENTIAL PARADIGMS (p. 35–41)

9. How are humanistic and existential paradigms similar to and different from psychoanalytic paradigms? Describe five assumptions underlying Carl Rogers' client-centered therapy. Describe three characteristics of Rogers' therapeutic intervention. (p. 35–37)

10. Describe three attitudes of existential therapists (look for (a) uncertainties of life, (b) anxiety and choice, (c) accepting responsibility). Describe two goals of existential therapy. Describe the basic goal of gestalt therapy. Describe five gestalt techniques and how each can help reach the basic goal. (p. 37–40)

11. Evaluate humanistic-existential paradigms by describing (a) two criticisms of their assumptions and (b) research on client-centered therapy. (p. 40–41)

LEARNING PARADIGMS (p. 41–49)

12. How did dissatisfaction with introspection lead to the rise of the learning paradigm? What are the assumptions of behaviorism as developed by Watson and others? Describe three conditioning models (classical, operant, and modeling) which developed out of behavioral assumptions. How did mediational learning paradigms modify behavioral assumptions? How did this modification expand the field? (p. 41–44)

13. Behavior therapy is characterized by what general approach? Briefly describe two examples of behavior therapies that developed out of each of the three conditioning models (six therapies in all). Evaluate learning paradigms by describing two issues. (p. 44–49)

THE COGNITIVE PARADIGM (p. 49–53)

14. What is the basic assumption of the cognitive paradigm (especially that cognition is "active")? How does past knowledge influence learning of new information? Describe the cognitive behavior therapy approaches of Ellis and of Beck. Evaluate the cognitive paradigm by discussing two basic issues. (p. 49–53)

CONSEQUENCES OF ADOPTING A PARADIGM/ECLECTICISM (p. 53–57)

15. How do paradigms have consequences for the ways researchers collect and interpret data — and for the arguments they get into? Describe the diathesis-stress paradigm as a way to make current paradigms more flexible. What are three key points of this approach? Finally, what does it mean to say that eclecticism in psychotherapy is common? (p. 53–57)

◆ SELF-TEST, CHAPTER 2

(* Items not covered in the Study Questions.)

MULTIPLE-CHOICE

1. Neurotransmitters
   a. deliver nerve impulse information between neurons.
   b. allow for the detection of brain activity, through measures such as EEG.
   c. transmit genetic information from parents to offspring.
   d. block the flow of information and contribute to behavioral problems.

2. The psychoanalytic paradigm rests upon the assumption that psychopathology is the result of
   a. incomplete superego development.
   b. unconscious conflicts.
   c. ego defense mechanisms.
   d. a breakdown of control over the pleasure principle.

3. Fixation at a particular stage, according to Freud, results in
   a. difficulties in determining the nature of the conflicts when the person enters analysis.
   b. a sexually unresponsive individual.
   c. an inability to develop further.
   d. regression to that stage when stressed later in life.

4. Defense mechanisms are produced by the _________, which is in the ___________.
   a. ego; unconscious
   b. superego; unconscious
   c. id; preconscious
   d. ego; conscious

5. A major emphasis of client-centered therapy is
   a. emphasizing self-actualization.
   b. unconditional positive regard.
   c. to improve awareness of one's own behavior.
   d. All of the above are correct.

6. As part of the behaviorism movement in psychology, there was a movement away from ________ techniques, and a movement toward _________ techniques for studying behavior.
   a. the case study; correlational studies
   b. phenomenology; operant conditioning
   c. introspection; direct observation
   d. determinism; the concept of free will

7. When you attempt to buy a soda from a machine, you only do so if the lights are on. According to Skinner, the lights on the soda machine are
   a. positive reinforcement.
   b. a discriminative stimulus.
   c. a signal for extinction.
   d. a conditioned stimulus.

8. Which paradigm argues that people interpret events selectively, and experience emotions based upon those interpretations?
   a. psychoanalytic paradigm
   b. cognitive paradigm
   c. learning paradigm
   d. diathesis-stress paradigm

9. The diathesis-stress paradigm emphasizes that abnormality results from
   a. biological factors and the unconscious.
   b. predisposition and current pressures.
   c. physiology and biochemistry.
   d. attachment and gestalt problems.

10. Contemporary psychologists primarily consider themselves
   a. eclectic.
   b. psychoanalytic or psychodynamic therapists.
   c. behavior therapists.
   d. cognitive or cognitive-behavior therapists.

SHORT ANSWER

1. According to behavioral genetics, what is the relationship between genes and abnormal behavior?

2. Why is "reductionism" a problem when developing theories?

3. What is contained in the collective unconscious according to Jung?

4. In psychoanalysis *why* is lifting repression considered desirable?

5. Identify four lasting contributions of Freud and psychoanalysis.

6. Identify a similarity and a difference between psychoanalysis and humanistic/existential paradigms.

7. Summarize the existential view about "choices" in people's lives.

8. Give two criticisms of humanistic approaches to therapy.

9. Behavior therapy is distinguished by what general approach to abnormality?

10. How would a therapist using Ellis' cognitive behavioral therapy deal with a college student who is anxious over grades?

◆ ANSWERS TO SELF-TEST, CHAPTER 2

MULTIPLE-CHOICE

1. a (p. 23)	2. b (p. 25)	3. d (p. 27)	4. a (p. 26, 28)
5. d (p. 36)	6. c (p. 41)	7. b (p. 43)	8. b (p. 49)
9. b (p. 55)	10. a (p. 57)		

SHORT ANSWER

1. Phenotypes (or observable behavior characteristics) result from interaction of environment and genotypes (unobservable, genetic influences). (p. 21)

2. Reductionistic explanations could be reduced again and again with no assurance the answers would apply to the original phenomena..(p. 25)

3. The understandings of our ancestors; experiences of humanity over the centuries. (p. 30)

4. So the patient can face the conflict and resolve it in light of adult reality. So the patient can recognize what motivates him or her and make better choices. (p. 30)

5. Importance of (a) childhood, (b) unconscious influences on behavior, (c) defense mechanisms, (d) non obvious factors in behavior. (p. 35)

6. Similar in emphasis on insight and awareness. Different in seeing human nature as asocial urges needing restraint vs. making choices, goodness, and growth. (p. 35–36)

7. Living involves anxiety-provoking choices. Growth comes from facing the anxiety and making the choices. (p. 37–38)

8. First: unclear that therapist can ever truly understand client's phenomenological world. Second: unclear that people are really good and able to solve own problems. (p. 40)

9. Epistemological stance of seeking rigorous proof. Application of experimental methods and knowledge. (p. 44)

10. Would challenge irrational beliefs about grades such as "I should always make A's" or "If I flunk out that would be terrible." (p. 51–52)

Chapter 3

Classification and Diagnosis

◆ OVERVIEW

This is the third of five introductory chapters. The first two chapters covered historical and contemporary paradigms or theories of abnormality. The remaining three chapters deal with less theoretical issues. Chapter 3 summarizes the standard diagnostic system for classifying disturbed individuals. It also discusses some basic issues regarding classification. Chapter 4 deals with issues and methods of assessment. Mental health professionals use these methods for both individual assessment and research. Chapter 5 will cover research methods and will complete the introductory chapters.

Chapters 3, 4, and 5 are less overtly theoretical than the earlier chapters. Still, the paradigm differences continue and are reflected in differences about how best to classify and study abnormality.

CHAPTER SUMMARY

Chapter 3 discusses the standard system for categorizing psychopathology and issues concerning this system as well as classification generally.

A Brief History of Classification describes early attempts to categorize abnormality and their development into the current system.

The Diagnostic System of the American Psychiatric Association (DSM-IV) summarizes some general characteristics of the current standard diagnostic system, especially its multiaxial classification approach. The chapter summarizes the main categories in DSM-IV. Later chapters will cover these categories in detail.

Issues in the Classification of Abnormal Behavior are (1) whether people should be classified at all and, (2) whether DSM-IV is a good classification system. In classifying, we lose information and may stigmatize people. However, some classification system is needed in order to study and treat problems. Earlier DSM systems were criticized for lack of reliability (consistency in applying labels) and validity (accuracy of the labels). DSM-IV appears more reliable but its broader utility is not yet clear.

TO MY STUDENTS

The disorders discussed in the text (beginning with Chapter 6) are primarily organized according to the classification system presented in Chapter 3. Study Chapter 3 carefully as it provides an overview of the labels and issues you will encounter later in the text.

ESSENTIAL CONCEPTS

1. Early classification systems did not clearly define disorders and were not widely accepted. Recent DSMs have provided extensive descriptions and clear reasons for label changes leading to wider acceptance.

2. The organization of mental disorders in the current DSM is the basis for organizing much of the text.

3. The current DSM-IV is multiaxial, inviting consideration of five axes or dimensions when making a diagnosis.

4. In DSM-IV problems are classified in sixteen major categories which are defined in this chapter.

5. Some critics object to the very concept of classifying abnormal behavior as we lose information and may stigmatize people. However, some system of distinguishing different problems seems needed.

6. DSM has been criticized for using discrete categories rather than dimensions or degrees of abnormality.

7. Earlier DSMs were criticized for low reliability (consistency of diagnosis) which limited their validity or accuracy.

8. DSM-IV contains specific diagnostic criteria and, as a result, has proven more reliable than its predecessors. However, its validity is uncertain and other problems remain.

KEY TERMS

Diagnostic and Statistical Manual of Mental Disorders (DSM) (p. 61)

Multiaxial classification (p. 62)

Categorical classification (p. 69)

Dimensional classification (p. 69)

Reliability (p. 71)

Interrater reliability (p. 71)

Construct validity (p. 72)

Disorders usually first diagnosed in infancy, childhood, or adolescence (p. 63)

Substance-related disorders (p. 63)

Schizophrenia (p. 63)

Mood disorders (p. 63)

Anxiety disorders (p. 63)

Somatoform disorders (p. 66)

Dissociative disorders (p. 66)

Sexual and gender identity disorders (p. 66)

Sleep disorders (p. 66)

Eating disorders (p. 66)

Factitious disorders (p. 66)

Adjustment disorders (p. 66)

Impulse control disorders (p. 66)

Personality disorders (p. 67)

Other conditions that may be the focus of clinical attention (p. 67)

Delirium, dementia, amnestic, and other cognitive disorders (p. 67)

◆ STUDY QUESTIONS

A BRIEF HISTORY OF CLASSIFICATION (p. 61–62)

1. What developments in other fields led to early interest in classifying abnormality? What was the problem with early classification systems? Identify two improvements of DSM systems beginning in 1988. (p. 61–62)

THE DIAGNOSTIC SYSTEM OF THE AMERICAN PSYCHIATRIC ASSOCIATION (DSM-IV) (p. 62–68)

2. What are the five axes in DSM-IV and the rationale for distinguishing them (especially axes I and II)? (p. 62)

3. Identify and define the major diagnostic categories involved in axes I and II (16 in all). (You may wish to refer to the glossary in the back of the text.) (p. 62–68)

ISSUES IN THE CLASSIFICATION OF ABNORMAL BEHAVIOR (p. 68–75)

4. Summarize two general criticisms of classification and the counterarguments to each. Despite these criticisms, what is the general value of classification and diagnosis? (p. 68–69)

5. Briefly identify three specific criticisms of diagnosis. (p. 69, 71, 72)

6. For the first criticism in question 5, distinguish between categorical and dimensional approaches. Give one reason that a dimensional system ought to be an improvement and two reasons it might not be one. (p. 69–71)

7. Define "reliability" and "validity." Explain them as issues in a classification system such as DSM. (p. 71–72)

8. Describe three things done to improve the reliability of recent DSMs. (p. 72–74)

9. What six problems remain in the DSM system? (p. 74–75)

◆ SELF-TEST, CHAPTER 3

(* Items not covered in Study Questions.)

MULTIPLE-CHOICE

1. In preparing the DSM-IV, working groups were formed for different classes of disorders to
   a. prepare literature reviews regarding disorders.
   b. collect additional data if necessary.
   c. analyze old data.
   d. All of the above are correct.

2. Axes I and II are distinguished
   a. so acute diagnoses may be emphasized on two axes.
   b. for greater precision in treatment.
   c. in order to account for enduring problems.
   d. to distinguish childhood and adult disorders.

3. John is difficult to understand when he speaks. Specifically, his comments are illogical, and he frequently shows signs of delusional ideas, such as the idea that his thoughts were placed there by someone else. What is the most likely diagnostic category for John based on this information?
   a. anxiety disorders
   b. schizophrenia
   c. dissociative disorders
   d. somatoform disorders

*4. Multiple personality disorder is just another name for
   a. schizophrenia.
   b. dissociative identity disorder.
   c. dissociative fugue.
   d. autism.

*5. Why does the DSM-IV include an appendix on diagnostic categories that have not yet been supported by sufficient data?
   a. to encourage researchers to study them
   b. to warn professionals familiar with earlier editions of the DSM not to continue using them
   c. to attract media attention
   d. to enable professionals to treat individuals not fitting one of the traditional diagnoses

6. Those arguing that labeling ignores the unique qualities of the individual would suggest that
   a. all diagnostic schemes should be avoided.
   b. the DSM is not the best approach to classification.
   c. classification procedures are unreliable and inaccurate.
   d. DSM criteria should be made more explicit.

7. An alternative to the DSM has been suggested where diagnoses are based upon
   a. exclusively theory-driven criteria.
   b. ratings along quantitative dimensions.
   c. an accumulation of symptoms that describe different diagnostic entities.
   d. None of the above choices have been suggested as alternatives to the DSM.

8. In order to study the reliability of a diagnostic category, we would study whether
   a. it acknowledges the uniqueness of each individual.
   b. it has explicitly stated criteria.
   c. patients with the label respond to treatment the same.
   d. diagnosticians apply it consistently.

9. Construct validity of a diagnosis refers to
   a. diagnoses that arise due to known medical factors.
   b. the consistency of diagnosing the same condition.
   c. whether accurate statements and predictions can be made about it.
   d. the likelihood that two diagnosticians would come up with the same diagnosis.

10. People diagnosed with schizophrenia usually respond well to haloperidol, whereas people with anxiety disorders do not. This is evidence for the _______________ of the diagnosis of schizophrenia.
   a. reliability
   b. validity
   c. categorical classification
   d. dimensional classification

SHORT ANSWER

1. What was the problem with early classification systems?

2. What are the characteristics of somatoform disorders in DSM-IV?

3. Define and give an example of "mood disorders."

4. The two major groups of issues regarding the classification of abnormal behavior are __________ and __________.

5. One possible criticism of current diagnostic practice is that it is difficult to indicate degrees of abnormality because . . .

6. A diagnostic label is __________ if diagnosticians agree on applying it to particular individuals.

7. Dr. Jones has just developed the new diagnostic label of "Sprangfordism." How will he demonstrate the construct validity of this label?

8. What was done to improve the reliability of recent DSMs?

9. In what way are diagnostic decision-making rules not clearly ideal in DSM?

10. According to the text, not all DSM classification changes seem positive. Explain.

◆ ANSWERS TO SELF-TEST, CHAPTER 3

MULTIPLE-CHOICE

1. d (p. 62)	2. c (p. 62)	3. b (p. 63)	4. b (p. 66)
5. a (p. 70)	6. a (p. 68)	7. b (p. 69)	8. d (p. 71)
9. c (p. 72)	10. b (p. 72)		

SHORT ANSWER

1. They had vague definitions and were not widely accepted. No consensus. (p. 61)

2. Physical symptoms that have a psychological, not a medical, cause. (p. 66)

3. Disturbances of mood or affect such as depression or mania. (p. 63)

4. General criticisms of classification, i.e., whether classification is useful and desirable, (and) criticisms of actual diagnostic practices, i.e., DSM. (p. 68–69)

5. The labels are discrete categorical entities (i.e., people either are or are not labeled). (p. 69)

6. Reliable (p. 71)

7. By showing that accurate statements can be made about people who receive the label. For example, they are different from others in their behavior, background, prognosis, response to treatment, etc. (p. 72)

8. Symptoms and criteria for making a diagnosis were defined more clearly and after considering cultural and other factors. (p. 72–73)

9. The rules seem arbitrary (why 3 of 6 characteristics rather than 2 or 4 of 6?). They still involve subjective judgments. (p. 74–75)

10. Too many problems, especially in children, were made into psychiatric disorders. (p. 75)

Chapter 4

Clinical Assessment Procedures

◆ OVERVIEW

This is the fourth of five introductory chapters covering basic issues in psychopathology. The first two chapters covered historical and contemporary paradigms or theories of abnormality. Chapter 3 dealt with DSM-IV, the standard system for classifying abnormality, and then went on to summarize general issues regarding classification.

This chapter discusses the major methods used to assess and classify behavior as well as issues underlying these methods. Many of these issues concern the accuracy of assessment methods. Other issues involve the paradigms discussed in Chapters 1 and 2.

Chapter 5 will cover research methods and will complete the introductory chapters. Research issues have been included in earlier chapters (and will appear throughout the text). Chapter 5 brings these issues together by showing the relative strengths and limitations of various research approaches.

Chapter 6 begins eleven chapters covering the various forms of abnormality. The last two chapters will cover related topics in abnormal psychology.

CHAPTER SUMMARY

Chapter 4 describes various methods and issues in assessing individuals and their problems. It discusses issues regarding the accuracy of assessments and describes methods of assessment. Not surprisingly, these methods are based on the various paradigms discussed in earlier chapters.

Reliability and Validity in Assessment describes ways of studying the reliability (or repeatability) and validity (or accuracy) of various approaches to assessment. These concepts are used in evaluating the assessment methods described in this chapter. Generally, reliability precedes validity. That is, techniques that are not reliable or repeatable cannot easily be accurate.

Psychological Assessment covers traditional assessment techniques of clinical interviews and psychological tests (including personality inventories, projective measures, and intelligence tests). It also describes assessment techniques developed out of the behavioral and cognitive paradigms.

Biological Assessment describes methods of assessing biological influences on behavior. Brain imaging and neurochemical methods examine the brain itself. Neuropsychological methods examine the effects of brain dysfunction on behavior. Psychophysiological methods examine bodily changes that accompany behavior including changes in sweating, breathing, and heart rate. Although these methods seem precise, they have difficulty accounting for how well individuals may adapt to neurological damage.

The last two sections of the chapter discuss important (and largely unanswered) issues in assessment. *Cultural Diversity and Clinical Assessment* discusses issues in assessing individuals of differing cultures. Studies suggest clinicians may misdiagnose pathology in individuals of other cultures. These studies suggest the need for great sensitivity and awareness of cultural variation.

The Consistency and Variability of Behavior reviews a basic argument over whether behavior is consistent or variable across situations. Traditional paradigms focus on personality traits leading to predictions that behavior will be consistent across situations. Behavioral paradigms and assessments suspect behavior varies with the situation.

ESSENTIAL CONCEPTS

1. Assessment methods are evaluated in terms of "reliability" and "validity." Methods must yield reliable or repeatable results before their validity or accuracy can be effectively studied.

2. Traditional psychological assessment methods include clinical interviews, personality inventories, projective techniques, and intelligence tests.

3. Clinical interviews can be useful in establishing rapport. They are often unstructured and results depend on the interviewer's skill, paradigm, etc.

4. Personality tests are standardized, structured self-report measures, but are limited by various problems of all self-report data.

5. Projective tests rely on individuals projecting their personality as they respond to ambiguous stimuli. The unstructured nature of these procedures has made them difficult to evaluate.

6. Intelligence tests predict academic potential with some success but can be misused and misinterpreted.

7. Although direct observation is the hallmark of behavioral assessment, self-report and cognitive measures are also used.

8. Biological assessment methods study the brain itself, behavioral effects of brain dysfunction, and physiological aspects of behavior. Each method has advantages but can be misinterpreted.

9. Psychologists are becoming aware of issues in assessing individuals from differing cultures. Insensitivity to cultural variation may lead to misdiagnosis.

10. Professionals continue to debate the degree to which behavior is determined by situations or by traits. This issue reflects differences between behavioral and more traditional paradigms.

KEY TERMS

Test-retest reliability (p. 77)

Alternate form reliability (p. 77)

Internal consistency reliability (p. 77)

Content validity (p. 78)

Criterion validity (p. 78)

Construct validity (p. 78)

Clinical interview (p. 79)

Structured interview (p. 80)

Psychological tests (p. 80)

Standardization (p. 80)

Personality inventory (p. 80)

Minnesota Multiphasic Personality Inventory [MMPI] (p. 80)

Projective test (p. 83)

Projective hypothesis (p. 83)

Rorschach inkblots (p. 84)

Thematic Apperception Test (p. 84)

Intelligence test (p. 85)

Behavioral observation (p. 87)

Self-monitoring (p. 88)

Ecological momentary assessment [EMA] (p. 88)

Reactivity [of behavior] (p. 89)

Meninges (p. 92)

Cerebral hemispheres (p. 92)

Corpus callosum (p. 92)

Cerebral cortex (p. 92)

Gyri (p. 92)

Sulci (p. 92)

Frontal lobe (p. 92)

Parietal lobe (p. 92)

Temporal lobe (p. 92)

Occipital lobe (p. 92)

White matter (p. 92)

Nuclei (p. 92)

Ventricles (p. 93)

Diencephalon (p. 93)

Thalamus (p. 93)

Hypothalamus (p. 93)

Midbrain (p. 93)

Brain stem (p. 93)

Pons (p. 93)

Medulla oblongata (p. 93)

Reticular formation (p. 93)

Cerebellum (p. 93)

Limbic system (p. 93)

CT scan (p. 93)

Magnetic resonance imaging [MRI] (p. 93)

Functional magnetic resonance imaging [fMRI] (p. 93)

PET scan (p. 94)

Neurologist (p. 95)

Neuropsychologist (p. 95)

Neuropsychological tests (p. 95)

Psychophysiology (p. 96)

Electrocardiogram (p. 97)

Electrodermal responding (p. 97)

Electroencephalogram (p. 97)

Somatic nervous system (p. 98)

Autonomic nervous system (ANS) (p. 98)

Sympathetic nervous system (p. 99)

Parasympathetic nervous system (p. 99)

◆ STUDY QUESTIONS

RELIABILITY AND VALIDITY IN ASSESSMENT (p. 77–78)

1. Define reliability and validity, and how the two are related. Briefly describe four types of reliability and three types of validity. (p. 77–78)

PSYCHOLOGICAL ASSESSMENT (p. 78–91)

2. Identify three general approaches to psychological assessment (on pages 79, 80, and 86). How are interviews similar to and different from normal conversation? Describe how four variables (paradigms, rapport, situational factors, and structure) influence interview results. (p. 79–80)

3. Identify three types of psychological tests (on pages 80, 83, 85). As an example of personality inventories, what was the MMPI designed to do? How was it developed and why was it revised? Briefly discuss the issue of faking on the MMPI. (p. 80–83)

4. What is the assumption underlying projective tests? How have they become more objective over the years? (p. 83–85)

5. What are intelligence tests designed to predict? What other uses do they have? Evaluate intelligence tests in terms of criterion validity and construct validity. (p. 85–86)

6. Distinguish between traditional and behavioral/cognitive assessment using the SORC acronym. Describe three approaches to behavioral and cognitive assessment using examples to illustrate the range of techniques. (p. 86–91)

BIOLOGICAL ASSESSMENT (p. 91–100)

7. Describe, with examples, three approaches to studying nervous system functioning. Identify advantages and disadvantages of each approach. (p. 91–96)

8. Describe, with examples, psychophysiological measurement. Identify a limitation of this approach. As a cautionary note, give two reasons to be cautious about biological assessment procedures generally. (p. 96–99)

CULTURAL DIVERSITY AND CLINICAL ASSESSMENT (p. 100–101)

9. What is the basic question regarding cultural diversity and clinical assessment? Give examples of clinicians under- and overpathologizing the problems of individuals from other cultures. What position does the text take on (a) being aware of cultural differences, and (b) including cultural differences in assessment? Identify four strategies for avoiding cultural bias in assessment. (p. 100–101)

THE CONSISTENCY AND VARIABILITY OF BEHAVIOR (p. 102–103)

10. Describe Mischel's (1968) position regarding the determinates of behavior and Wachtel's three counterpoints. Summarize the debate, including flaws in studies, self-report questionnaires, and functionality of behavior. What is the text's conclusion? (p. 102–103)

◆ SELF-TEST, CHAPTER 4

(* Items not covered in Study Questions.)

MULTIPLE-CHOICE

1. Diane was taking a personality test. The test has items that are all closely related to one another. This is an example of
   a. external validity.
   b. internal consistency.
   c. internal validity.
   d. test-retest reliability.

2. The MMPI is an example of a(n)
   a. projective test.
   b. personality inventory.
   c. intelligence test.
   d. structured clinical interview.

3. The projective hypothesis assumes which of the following?
   a. Responses to highly structured tasks reveal hidden attitudes and motivations.
   b. Preferences for unstructured stimuli reveal unconscious motives.
   c. Unstructured stimuli provoke anxiety.
   d. Responses to ambiguous stimuli are influenced by unconscious factors.

4. The construct validity of intelligence tests is limited by
   a. how psychologists define intelligence.
   b. the nature of the population tested with the instruments.
   c. their generally low reliability.
   d. None of the above choices are correct.

5. Which of the following is *least* likely to be used in behavioral assessment?
   a. projective tests
   b. clinical interviews
   c. self-report inventories
   d. physiological measures

6. When Liz is in the supermarket, she feels increasing anxiety, and she then says to herself, "I just can't stand feeling this feeling." Her self-statement would be the
   a. S.
   b. O.
   c. R.
   d. C.

*7. It was found through a brain scan that a man had higher than normal levels of activity in his limbic system. This man probably was having difficulty with
   a. physical movement of the body.
   b. regulation of sleep and arousal.
   c. regulation of emotion.
   d. language formation.

8. Functional MRI (fMRI) differs from ordinary MRI in that
   a. fMRI can record metabolic changes in the brain.
   b. ordinary MRI can only be done annually.
   c. fMRI relies upon other tests to assess brain function.
   d. ordinary MRI is invasive.

*9. Two people the same age, Sarah and Linda, were administered the Luria-Nebraska neuropsychological test battery. Sarah graduated with a Ph.D., while Linda did not complete high school. Assuming all other factors equal, the scores they receive on the Luria-Nebraska
   a. should differ. Sarah should score higher based on education.
   b. should differ. Linda should score higher as it is not based on education.
   c. should not differ since the test controls for education level.
   d. It is impossible to predict the differences.

10. Cultural diversity should lead clinicians to
   a. avoid using most tests with individuals from other cultures.
   b. adhere strictly to DSM criteria in making diagnoses.
   c. be especially alert for pathological behavior that is acceptable in another culture.
   d. seek information on various cultural practices and views.

SHORT ANSWER

1. How are reliability and validity related?

2. Identify one similarity and one difference between normal conversation and clinical interviews.

3. What type of items are used in lie scales of personality inventories such as the MMPI?

4. How have projective tests become more objective over the years?

5. What are intelligence tests designed to measure or predict?

6. Dr. Jones is a behavioral psychologist helping the Smiths, who are having "discipline problems" with their child. Dr. Jones would like to directly observe this behavior without having to spend several days in the Smiths' home waiting for it to occur. What can Dr. Jones do?

7. What is an advantage of neuropsychological assessment over other biological assessment procedures such as brain imaging?

8. In general what are the limitations of biological measures of behavior?

9. Why can *over*sensitivity to cultural issues among clinicians be a problem?

10. Why is Mischel's position on behavioral consistency less applicable in clinical situations according to some critics?

◆ ANSWERS TO SELF-TEST, CHAPTER 4

MULTIPLE-CHOICE

1. b (p. 77–78)	2. b (p. 80)	3. d (p. 83)	4. a (p. 86)
5. a (p. 87)	6. b (p. 86–87)	7. c (p. 93)	8. a (p. 93–94)
9. c (p. 96)	10. d (p. 100)		

SHORT ANSWER

1. Reliability limits validity. A measure that is not reliable (repeatable) cannot easily be valid (accurate or correct). (p. 78)

2. Similar as both are ways of finding out about others. Different in that interviews only seek information about one person, the interviewee, and pay attention to *how* the interviewee says things. (p. 79)

3. Items that people might like to endorse but cannot do honestly. (p. 83)

4. More objective, standardized scoring methods have been developed. (p. 65)

5. Who will succeed in school. (p. 85)

6. Have the Smiths interact with their child in the consulting room while Dr. Jones observes. (p. 87)

7. Can detect more subtle changes by looking at how the brain functions rather than changes in its structure. (p. 95)

8. Are influenced by how well a person has adjusted to damage and his or her initial abilities as well as limitations of instruments and our knowledge of brain. (p. 99–100)

9. Oversensitivity may lead clinicians to minimize the seriousness of problems by attributing them to subcultural norms. (p. 100–101)

10. Clinically disturbed individuals may be more consistent in behavior than Mischel suggests. In fact, their problem may be that they are insensitive (or overly sensitive) to situations. (p. 102)

Chapter 5

Research Methods in the Study of Abnormal Behavior

◆ OVERVIEW

Earlier chapters have covered paradigms or theories in psychopathology (Chapters 1 and 2) and classification and assessment issues (Chapters 3 and 4). Chapter 5 discusses scientific methods and research designs in abnormal psychology.

Many research issues have already been mentioned in Chapters 1 through 4. At times it may have seemed that scientific research creates more confusion than answers. Research can be complex, at least in part because scientists are very concerned about the limitations of their approach and their methods. It is said that there is no perfect research design. Each has both strengths and limitations. Chapter 5 describes these strengths and limitations as a basis for understanding research into the various problem behaviors discussed later in the text.

Chapter 5 is the last introductory chapter. Chapter 6 is the first of eleven chapters, comprising parts two and three of the text, discussing the various specific forms of abnormality. Chapters 6 and 7 cover problems related directly or indirectly to anxiety. These disorders used to be referred to as neuroses.

CHAPTER SUMMARY

Chapter 5 discusses the methods scientists use to develop systematic knowledge as a basis for developing and evaluating theories and principles.

Science and Scientific Methods discusses basic principles of science. Statements and ideas must be publicly testable and capable of being proven false. Observations must be reliable or repeatable. Theories are propositions that both result from research and generate testable ideas for further research.

The Research Methods of Abnormal Psychology include case studies, epidemiological research, correlational studies, experiments, single-subject and mixed designs. Each method has advantages and disadvantages. They vary in the kinds of data they produce and the kinds of inferences, especially about causation, which can be drawn.

The case study is an extensive description of a particular, often unusual, problem or procedure. It is difficult to develop general principles from them, but they can provide examples to disconfirm principles and generate ideas for further research.

Epidemiological research studies how an illness or characteristic is distributed across the population. Such studies can be helpful in planning treatment needs as well as suggesting possible causes for a problem.

Correlational methods measure the relationship between two (or more) variables (for example, between course grades and anxiety). They are widely used in abnormal psychology but, because they do not actually manipulate variables, it is difficult to draw conclusions about causation from them.

In experiments one (or more) independent variables are actually manipulated and the effects of the change on dependent variable(s) are studied. Experiments are preferred for studying causation. However, in abnormal psychology, many variables cannot be manipulated for practical or ethical reasons. Experiments seek internal validity by using procedures such as control groups and random assignment. External validity is difficult with any research design.

The single-subject ABAB design studies the effect on a single individual's behavior of repeatedly (a) holding back and, (b) applying some manipulation. This design can produce dramatic effects although generalizability is difficult.

Mixed designs combine correlational and experimental techniques by actively manipulating only some variables.

ESSENTIAL CONCEPTS

1. Science is the pursuit of systematized knowledge through observation, although it is not purely objective and is influenced by the paradigms of the researcher and of society.

2. In order to be considered scientific, ideas must be publicly testable, and reliable or repeatable.

3. Scientific theories both account for data and generate hypotheses. Theoretical concepts bridge spatial and temporal relations and summarize observed relations.

4. The case study lacks control and objectivity, but it can be useful for (a) describing unusual phenomena, (b) disconfirming supposedly universal aspects of a theory, and (c) generating hypotheses.

5. Epidemiological research investigates the frequency and distribution of some problem or variable in the population. Such research is useful for social planning and can suggest causes of a problem.

6. Correlational methods study the degree of association between two or more variables (for example, IQ and grades). The variables are only observed, not manipulated. Thus, directionality and third-variable problems are difficult to answer and causal inferences are risky.

7. Statistical significance refers to a convention adopted by scientists wherein a finding is not considered to be meaningful unless the odds are less than 5 in 100 that it occurred by chance.

8. An experiment differs from a correlational method because one of the variables is actively manipulated. When properly conducted, an experiment is a powerful tool to study causality but ethical and practical problems often limit its use in studying psychopathology.

9. The basic features of an experiment include the experimental hypothesis, independent variables, dependent variables, and experimental effects.

10. Internal validity refers to whether the results obtained can be confidently attributed to the independent variable. Internal validity is aided by control groups and random assignment to eliminate confounds. There is debate over the role of placebo controls in psychological research.

11. External validity concerns generalizability of a particular study. It is difficult to evaluate.

12. Analogue experiments are frequently used to study psychopathology but their external validity is always of concern.

13. Single-subject research can dramatically demonstrate a phenomenon in one subject although generalizability is a problem.

14. Mixed designs study the effect of several variables, some of which are observed (as in correlational methods) and some of which are actually manipulated (as in the experiment).

KEY TERMS

Science (p. 106)

Theory (p. 106)

Case study (p. 109)

Epidemiology (p. 111)

Prevalence (p. 111)

Incidence (p. 111)

Risk factors (p. 111)

Lifetime prevalence rates (p. 112)

Correlational method (p. 112)

Correlation coefficient [r] (p. 113)

Statistical significance (p. 114)

Classificatory variables (p. 115)

Directionality problem (p. 115)

High-risk method (p. 115)

Third-variable problem (p. 116)

The experiment (p. 116)

Experimental hypothesis (p. 117)

Independent variable (p. 117)

Random assignment (p. 117)

Dependent variable (p. 117)

Experimental effect (p. 117)

Control group (p. 117)

Confounds (p. 118)

Internal validity (p. 118)

Placebo effect (p. 118)

Placebo control group (p. 119)

Double-blind procedure (p. 119)

External validity (p. 120)

Analogue experiment (p. 120)

Single-subject experimental design (p. 121)

Reversal [ABAB] design (p. 122)

Mixed design (p. 122)

Meta-analysis (p. 124)

◆ STUDY QUESTIONS

SCIENCE AND SCIENTIFIC METHODS (p. 106–109)

1. Describe two basic requirements of any scientific approach. Identify two roles of theory. In constructing theories, what are two advantages of theoretically inferred concepts and two views on judging the legitimacy of theoretical concepts? (p. 106–109)

THE RESEARCH METHODS OF ABNORMAL PSYCHOLOGY (p. 109–123)

2. List six research methods of abnormal psychology (on pages 109 to 122). What is done in a case study (the first method)? Describe three ways in which case studies are useful. (p. 109–111)

3. What is epidemiology? Describe two uses of epidemiological research in psychopathology. (p. 111–112)

4. What are correlational methods and how are they different from experimental research? How are correlations measured and their significance evaluated? (p. 112–114)

5. Why are correlational methods often used in studying psychopathology? What is their major drawback and two reasons for it? (p. 114–116)

6. How does the experiment overcome the drawback of correlational methods? Identify five basic features of the experimental design. How is the significance of an experimental effect determined? (p. 116–117)

7. What is internal validity? Describe how control groups and random assignment are used to eliminate confounds and provide internal validity. (p. 117–118)

8. In psychotherapy research, how are placebo effects viewed and controlled? Describe issues in using placebo controls in psychotherapy research. What is external validity and why is it difficult to demonstrate? (p. 118–120)

9. What are analogue experiments? What is an advantage and a disadvantage of using analogues in experimental designs? (p. 120–121)

10. What is the single-subject ABAB design and how does it show that the manipulation produced the result? What is the primary disadvantage of this design? (p. 121–122)

11. What is a mixed design? Give examples, explaining why they are mixed designs. Identify an advantage and a disadvantage of mixed designs. (p. 122–123)

◆ SELF-TEST, CHAPTER 5

(* Items not covered in Study Questions.)

MULTIPLE-CHOICE

1. Frequently, theories are developed by
   a. sudden insight.
   b. determining the most useful way to look at a set of data.
   c. pondering the implications of a paradigm.
   d. all of the above choices are correct.

2. Dr. Roberts noted that whenever her student, Ted, was given praise for reading, he read more. She then stated that reinforcement increases his behavior. Using this framework, ______ is a theoretical concept, whereas _______ was derived from the theory to illustrate the concept.
   a. reading; praise
   b. reinforcement; praise
   c. reading; behavior
   d. reinforcement; reinforcement

3. Dr. Lee has been treating someone with an unusual combination of symptoms. He notes that there are no published studies on such a combination of symptoms, and considers developing a case study. How would Dr. Lee conduct this study?
   a. Try to find other cases like the one he is treating.
   b. Gather detailed historical and biographical information on this single individual.
   c. Examine treatment response using an ABAB design.
   d. Withhold treatment in an effort to fully understand the significance of symptoms.

4. Epidemiology is the study of
   a. unique cases or unusual disorders.
   b. the rates and correlates of disorders in a population.
   c. the development of disorders over the life span.
   d. mental disorders in other cultures.

5. Correlational research differs from experimental research in that correlational research
   a. is associated with external validity.
   b. does not involve manipulation of variables.
   c. relies on significance tests.
   d. samples large groups of participants.

6. Statistical significance in research suggests the results are
   a. internally valid.
   b. externally valid.
   c. not affected by experimenter bias.
   d. not due to chance.

7. Psychopathologists rely upon correlational research because
   a. it is effective in determining cause and effect.
   b. many of the variables they wish to study cannot be manipulated.
   c. ethical considerations prevent them from doing case studies.
   d. they do not have access to large samples of disordered individuals.

8. Dr. Wilhelm randomly assigned 50 depressed patients (half women and half men) to two groups for treatment. One group received medication, and the other received cognitive therapy. Ratings of the depression level of the subjects were taken before and after treatment. The rating of subjects' depression level is the
   a. dependent variable.
   b. confound variable.
   c. third variable.
   d. independent variable.

9. Mary, who has trichotillomania (chronic hair pulling) is using an ABAB design to see if she pulls more hair while watching TV. She watched TV during dinner for four weeks and pulled at least ten hairs a day for the four weeks. Then she left the TV off for four weeks and pulled only one hair per day for the four weeks. In the next step of this design, Mary should
   a. get other subjects to follow the same procedure.
   b. have her mother rate how much she eats.
   c. turn the TV back on for four weeks.
   d. change what she eats during dinner.

10. Mixed designs are most useful in
   a. determining cause and effect.
   b. identifying which particular treatment is best for which group of patients.
   c. examining relations between disorders and prevalence.
   d. obtaining internally valid results.

SHORT ANSWER

1. Young Sigmund Freud was amazed at the number of his clients who reported being sexually abused as children. He could not believe sexual abuse was that common so he developed the oedipal conflict. This is an example of theory building by using _____ in order to _____ .

2. Explain how case studies can be used to disprove general theories.

3. What kind of research design would be used to identify reasons that college students drop out of school?

4. Explain the "directionality problem" in correlational research.

5. Experiments are said to be internally valid if . . .

6. Professor Diaz finds that females get better scores than males on his essay tests. He would like to prove that this happens because they give better answers — not because of sexual bias on his part. Describe a double-blind procedure he could use to do this.

7. Why is it difficult to demonstrate external validity?

8. What factors determine whether a research study is an analogue study?

9. In a single-subject ABAB design, how can we be sure that the manipulation produced the result?

10. Give an example of a mixed research design.

◆ ANSWERS TO SELF-TEST, CHAPTER 5

MULTIPLE-CHOICE

1. a (p. 106)	2. b (p. 107)	3. b (p. 109)	4. b (p. 111)
5. b (p. 112–116)	6. d (p. 114)	7. b (p. 114–115)	8. a (p. 117)
9. c (p. 122)	10. b (p. 123)		

SHORT ANSWER

1. (using) an inferred theoretical concept (in order to) bridge spatiotemporal relations. (p. 107)

2. By providing a clear example which doesn't work as the theory predicts. (p. 110–111)

3. Epidemiological research. (p. 112)

4. Correlations show that two variables are related but do not show which variable leads to the other. For example IQ and school grades correlate, which could mean that smart people get better grades or that people who are taught more in school become smarter. (p. 115)

5. The effect can be confidently attributed to manipulating the independent variable. (p. 117–118)

6. Professor Diaz could have someone else, who will not be involved in grading the tests, remove all names and identifying information from the test papers before he scores them. (p. 119)

7. There is no way to know for sure to what situations results will generalize. The best one can do is perform similar experiments in new situations. (p. 120)

8. How the results are used. What implications are made or what other situations the results are applied to. (p. 120)

9. By reversing (introducing and removing) the independent variable repeatedly. When the behavior repeatedly changes along with the independent variable, we can feel confident that the manipulation produced the change. (p. 122)

10. Your example should include two independent variables, one of which is simply measured (a classificatory variable) and one of which is manipulated. For example: compare test scores of male and female students (a classificatory variable) after they spend two hours hearing a lecture or reading the text (a manipulation). (p. 122)

Chapter 6

Anxiety Disorders

◆ OVERVIEW

The first five chapters have discussed a number of basic ideas and issues in abnormal psychology. These concepts provide a framework for surveying the various forms of abnormality. You will want to refer back to these chapters periodically as you study the rest of the text.

The next eleven chapters survey the various forms of abnormality. Now would be a good time to glance over all these chapters. Notice that they cover a wide range of problem behaviors. A number of them are matters of current social debate. After covering forms of abnormality, the last two chapters in the text discuss issues in intervention as well as legal and ethical issues.

The first two chapters on forms of abnormality, Chapters 6 and 7, discuss problems related directly or indirectly to anxiety. Chapter 6 covers anxiety disorders which more or less directly involve excessive fears, worries, and anxiety. Chapter 7 discusses two groups of problems where anxiety may be more subtly involved. They are somatoform disorders, characterized by physical symptoms or complaints, and dissociative disorders, involving disturbances in memory and awareness. Although the traditional psychoanalytic term "neurosis" is no longer used to describe these problems, anxiety is still seen as involved in various ways.

Chapters 8 and 9 look at other problems that also involve anxiety but in which physical and medical issues are more prominent. Chapter 8 discusses stress effects on general health as well as on psychophysiological disorders, such as ulcers and heart conditions, which have long been recognized as involving anxiety and stress. Chapter 9 focuses on eating disorders, such as anorexia nervosa, which involve health problems resulting from cultural and other stresses.

CHAPTER SUMMARY

Chapter 6 begins the survey of psychological problems by discussing anxiety disorders. In studying the chapter, look for the format described in "To My Students" below. Five kinds of anxiety disorders are discussed.

Phobias are relatively common disorders involving intense, unreasonable, disruptive fears of particular situations. They include (a) specific phobias such as fear of snakes and (b) social phobias such as fear of public embarrassment. Psychoanalysts view phobias as defenses against repressed conflicts. Behaviorists have offered avoidance, modeling and prepared learning models for the development of phobias. These models, as well as cognitive and biological approaches, have led to treatment approaches.

Panic Disorder involves sudden, unexpected attacks of anxiety. Panic attacks may lead to agoraphobia or fear of leaving safe places. Research suggests that these people escalate stressors into full-blown panic due to their fear-of-fear or fear of loss of control. People with *Generalized Anxiety Disorder* live in relatively constant tension. People with *Obsessive-compulsive Disorders* are bothered by unwanted thoughts (obsessions) and/or feel compelled to engage in repetitive rituals (compulsions) lest they be overcome by anxiety. There are a variety of psychoanalytic, behavioral, cognitive, and biological views on the cause of each disorder that have led to corresponding treatments.

Posttraumatic Stress Disorder reflects a recognition that traumatic events such as disasters or combat may affect anyone. Aftereffects include reexperiencing the traumatic event, avoiding stimuli associated with the event, and increased arousal. Treatments emphasize rapid intervention, and talking through or reliving the event in a supportive atmosphere.

ESSENTIAL CONCEPTS

1. Anxiety disorders used to be called neuroses based on the psychoanalytic view that anxiety is caused by unconscious conflict.

2. The major categories of anxiety disorders listed in DSM-IV are: phobias, panic disorder, generalized anxiety disorder, obsessive-compulsive disorder, and posttraumatic stress disorder.

3. A phobia is a disrupting, fear-mediated avoidance, out of proportion to the actual danger from the object or situation that is feared.

4. Psychoanalytic, behavioral, cognitive, and biological models of phobias have been proposed. None account for all phobias. A diathesis model allows for consideration of multiple factors to account more fully for phobias.

5. Various therapies for phobias all emphasize reexperiencing the feared situation. Drugs have also been used but are typically effective only so long as the person continues to take them.

6. Panic disorders, involving unexpected attacks of anxiety, may lead to agoraphobia or fear of public places. Several biological and psychological approaches exist.

7. Generalized anxiety disorder, characterized by chronic anxiety, has often been viewed and treated in ways similar to phobias. Treatment approaches seek to help people manage their fears in various ways.

8. Obsessive-compulsive disorder involves obsessive thoughts and compulsive behaviors. A wide range of causes and treatments have been proposed with limited success.

9. Posttraumatic stress disorder (PTSD) is, primarily, an aftereffect of experiencing trauma, although other factors increase the risk of PTSD after a trauma.

10. PTSD is treated various ways. Typically treatment stresses immediate intervention, exposure under supportive conditions, and social support.

To My Students

This is the first of many chapters covering specific psychological disorders. As you study them you will discover that each follows the same general outline. First, the problem is defined and any issues regarding its classification in DSM-IV are discussed. Second, theories and research into its causes are described. Typically these include the Psychoanalytic, Behavioral, Cognitive, and Biological paradigms. Finally, various treatments are summarized using the same paradigms. Of course the outline varies, but you will find it helpful to look for this kind of outline as you study each chapter and to organize your studying around it.

This is also a good time to warn you of a common experience among students studying abnormal psychology. Often, students in these courses come to believe they have the problem covered in each chapter. For example, you may think you have an anxiety disorder when studying Chapter 6, depression in Chapter 10, and schizophrenia in Chapter 11. If this happens to you, don't be surprised. The various problems covered in the text are exaggerations of very normal tendencies in all of us. If you can see these tendencies in yourself, it probably means you have developed a meaningful understanding of the problem. Of course, if you are seriously concerned, you can discuss the matter with your instructor or someone at your school's counseling center. They are used to such situations and you may be surprised at how easily they understand your concerns.

KEY TERMS

Anxiety (p. 127)

Neuroses (p. 127)

Anxiety disorders (p. 127)

Comorbidity (p. 127)

Phobia (p. 128)

Specific phobias (p. 129)

Social phobia (p. 129)

Vicarious learning (p. 131)

Autonomic lability (p. 134)

Flooding (p. 135)

Anxiolytics (p. 136)

Panic disorder (p. 137)

Depersonalization (p. 137)

Derealization (p. 137)

Agoraphobia (p. 137)

School phobia (p. 138)

Elective mutism (p. 138)

Generalized anxiety disorder [GAD] (p. 143)

Obsessive-compulsive disorder [OCD] (p. 146)

Obsessions (p. 146)

Compulsion (p. 146)

Posttraumatic stress disorder [PTSD] (p. 151)

Acute stress disorder (p. 152)

◆ STUDY QUESTIONS

1. Define "neuroses" pointing out the theoretical assumptions involved. How have recent DSMs dealt with this term? Identify three reasons for comorbidity. (p. 127–128)

PHOBIAS (p. 128–137)

2. What are phobias and why do psychoanalysts (but not behaviorists) focus on their content? Describe two types of phobias. Summarize the Freudian theory of phobias. Summarize three behavioral theories of phobias. (p. 128–132)

3. What is the general limitation of behavioral theories and why would it be helpful to add the idea of "diatheses" to them? Describe four possible diatheses for phobias (social skills, cognitive, autonomic, genetic). (p. 132–134)

4. Summarize the (a) psychoanalytic, (b) behavioral (five techniques), and (c) cognitive approaches to therapy for phobias. What do all these techniques have in common? What is the key problem with the common biological treatment? (p. 134–137)

PANIC DISORDER (p. 137–143)

5. Describe the characteristics of panic disorder and its relation to agoraphobia. Evaluate four biological and two psychological factors or hypotheses about panic disorder. (p.137–142)

6. Identify three disadvantages to biological treatments for panic disorders. Describe two general psychological treatments and compare their effectiveness to biological treatments. (p. 142–143)

GENERALIZED ANXIETY DISORDER (p. 143–146)

7. Describe the characteristics of generalized anxiety disorder. Summarize the psychoanalytic, four cognitive-behavioral, and two biological views on its cause. (p. 143–144)

8. Summarize four cognitive-behavioral components in treatment of GAD. Compare the effectiveness of these approaches to drug therapies. Identify the advantages and disadvantages of drug therapies. (p. 144–146)

OBSESSIVE-COMPULSIVE DISORDER (p. 146–151)

9. Define and give several examples of obsessions and of compulsions. How are these definitions different from the way we commonly use the terms? Summarize views on the causes of obsessive-compulsive disorders (two psychoanalytic, three behavioral and cognitive, and three biological views). (p. 146–149)

10. Briefly summarize five treatments for obsessive-compulsive disorders (including two biological treatments). How effective are treatments for OCD generally? (p. 149–151)

POSTTRAUMATIC STRESS DISORDER (p. 151–158)

11. How is posttraumatic stress disorder (PTSD) defined differently from most disorders? Describe three main characteristics of PTSD. Describe risk factors for PTSD including severity of trauma, dissociative symptoms, and coping style. Describe three theories of its cause. (p. 151–154)

12. Identify two basic principles in treating PTSD. Describe two early approaches to treating veterans with PTSD and the current general approach. Describe three variations on this idea and the use of drugs. (p. 154–158)

◆ SELF-TEST, CHAPTER 6

(* Items not covered in Study Questions.)

MULTIPLE-CHOICE

1. Which of the following is a reason for comorbidity among anxiety disorders?
   a. Often anxiety disorder sufferers are so impaired that they develop additional syndromes.
   b. Many symptoms of anxiety disorders are not exclusively specific to that disorder.
   c. Anxiety is part of almost all psychopathology.
   d. Anxiety is part of a continuum of a variety of disorders.

2. Margaret and Ed have different fears. Margaret is afraid of snakes, whereas Ed is afraid of dogs. Their fears are similar in that
   a. both likely have a similar function.
   b. both require aversive learning consequences for their development.
   c. neither respond well to treatment.
   d. All of the above choices are correct.

3. Jim was bitten by a goose when he was a child. Now, as an adult, when he goes to ponds where geese flock, he experiences fear and leaves. His anxiety subsides once he leaves. This illustrates the _______________ theory of phobias.
   a. two-factor
   b. psychoanalytic
   c. learning
   d. cognitive

4. After viewing tapes of monkeys apparently showing fear of snakes, lambs, and flowers, monkeys who viewed these tapes were only fearful of snakes. This provides only partial support for ________ but better support for ________.
   a. modeling; classical conditioning
   b. vicarious learning; avoidance learning
   c. modeling; preparedness
   d. preparedness; diathesis

5. Cognitive therapy for the treatment of specific phobias is limited by the fact that
   a. some patients have difficulty becoming deeply relaxed.
   b. phobics often become too frightened to discuss their fears directly.
   c. many fears are based on real experiences and thus are not in fact irrational.
   d. phobics already recognize that their fears are unreasonable.

*6. Alexandra has school phobia. Which of the following is *most likely* also true regarding Alexandra?
   a. She has been abused.
   b. She has a learning disability.
   c. Her mother refused to go to school when she was young.
   d. She has a health problem.

7. A problem in research that involves creating panics in the lab by hyperventilation has been
   a. convincing panickers to hyperventilate when they are not experiencing a panic.
   b. the low rate of hyperventilation during naturally occurring panics.
   c. an inability to create panics even after long durations of hyperventilation.
   d. inexact amounts of carbon dioxide inhalation.

8. What diagnosis is most appropriate for Nicole? She is constantly concerned with symmetry, often spending hours arranging items in her room so that the room appears even on the left and right. She also feels that when she eats, the items on the plate must be arranged symmetrically. All of this effort interferes with her work.
   a. Obsessive-compulsive disorder
   b. Obsessive-compulsive personality disorder
   c. Generalized anxiety disorder
   d. Specific phobia

*9. The controversy surrounding posttraumatic stress disorder (PTSD) has been that
   a. most people recover from PTSD within one month.
   b. most people do not develop PTSD after experiencing trauma.
   c. the definition of a traumatic event is so broad as to include almost any stressful human experience.
   d. All of the above.

10. Current psychological treatments for PTSD all emphasize
   a. talking out feelings about the event in a supportive group.
   b. reassurance and rest until memories become less painful.
   c. encouragement to resume normal functioning.
   d. exposure to the traumatic event.

SHORT ANSWER

1. What assumption was the basis for the term "neurosis"?

2. Define "social phobia," distinguishing it from specific phobias.

3. Cognitive research suggests what basis for phobias?

4. Describe what is done in systematic desensitization as a treatment for phobias.

5. In what way are panic disorder and generalized anxiety disorder similar?

6. What is the basis for generalized anxiety according to the psychoanalytic view?

7. Mary is chronically anxious. She is very shy and awkward around others. She reports feeling that she can't do anything right. What would a behavioral therapist do to help Mary?

8. What is the distinction between obsessions and compulsions?

9. How is PTSD defined differently from most disorders?

10. What topics are commonly discussed in rap sessions held to help Vietnam veterans deal with stress reactions?

◆ ANSWERS TO SELF-TEST, CHAPTER 6

MULTIPLE-CHOICE

1. b (p. 127)	2. a (p. 129)	3. a (p. 131)	4. c (p. 131–132)
5. d (p. 136)	6. c (p. 138)	7. b (p. 140)	8. a (p. 147)
9. b (p. 151–152)	10. d (p. 156)		

SHORT ANSWER

1. Freudian assumption that many problems were based, directly or indirectly, on repressed anxiety. (p. 127)

2. Unreasonable fears tied to presence of others, public situations, etc. Specific phobias involve specific situations. Social phobia involves a wide range of situations. (p. 129–130)

3. Phobic individuals attend to negative events and believe they will reoccur. They focus on future fear-inducing possibilities. (p. 133)

4. Individual is taught how to relax deeply. Then, while relaxed, the person experiences (perhaps, by imagining them) a series of gradually more fearful situations. (p. 135)

5. Person experiences anxiety which is *not* linked to a particular situation. (p. 137, 143)

6. Conflicts and impulses that have been repressed. The individual is afraid but does not know what he or she is afraid of because it is repressed. Thus, the fear is chronic. (p. 143)

7. Behaviorist would see her anxiety as tied to social fears (a social phobia or cued fear). Relaxation, assertiveness, and social skills training may be appropriate. (p. 144–145)

8. Obsessions are thoughts and compulsions are behaviors. (p. 146)

9. The cause or etiology is part of the definition. (p. 151)

10. Feelings about the war (guilt, anger), about family life (social and family changes), and society's attitudes toward the war. (p. 155)

Chapter 7

Somatoform and Dissociative Disorders

◆ OVERVIEW

Chapter 7 is the second chapter on disorders related to anxiety and stress. The previous chapter discussed disorders involving fairly direct expressions of anxiety. These included chronic anxiety, phobias or unreasonable fears, and obsessions and compulsions in which people think and do things in order to control anxiety. Chapter 7 describes disorders in which people may not directly complain of anxiety but have other problems that appear related to anxiety and stress in some way. These are somatoform disorders (involving physical complaints) and dissociative disorders (involving altered memory and awareness). Both arise from psychological factors such as anxiety and stress.

After this, Chapters 8 and 9 discuss how anxiety and stress can lead to illness and physical or tissue changes. Traditionally, we have recognized the role of stress in psychophysiological disorders such as ulcers. However, we now recognize that stress can play a role in virtually all physical/medical problems. Chapter 8 discusses both these roles. Chapter 9 discusses eating disorders, such as anorexia nervosa, which also involve anxiety and physical problems. However, eating disorders also involve significant social and cultural issues.

CHAPTER SUMMARY

Chapter 7 covers two groups of disorders in which there is a loss of functioning with no physical basis. The symptoms seem to serve a psychological purpose.

Somatoform Disorders are characterized by physical complaints that have no physiological basis. The text emphasizes two of these disorders. In conversion disorder there is a loss of sensory or motor functioning: for example a loss of vision, touch, etc., or of the ability to walk, talk, etc. In somatization disorder there are multiple physical complaints (headaches, various pains, fatigue, etc.) typically involving repeated visits to physicians and medical treatment.

Knowledge about somatoform disorders is limited because individuals with these problems typically seek medical, not psychological, treatment. Existing theories deal primarily with conversions. Psychoanalysts propose that repressed conflicts are "converted" into the physical symptoms in various ways and seek to uncover what was repressed. Behavioral theorists suggest that the behaviors reduce anxiety and seek to teach more effective behaviors.

Dissociative Disorders are disorders of awareness and memory. In dissociative amnesia, the individual is unable to recall important personal information, often of traumatic events.

Dissociative fugue involves a more encompassing memory loss in which the person leaves home and assumes a new identity. Depersonalization disorder is characterized by disconcerting alternations in perception of the self. In dissociative identity disorder (DID), two or more separate and distinct personalities occur in alternation, each having its own memories, behaviors, and life styles.

Psychological theories propose that memory losses in dissociative disorders protect the individual from traumatic memories, perhaps of childhood abuse. Another theory suggests they are learned social roles. Because these disorders strongly suggest repression, psychoanalytic techniques are often used in treatment.

ESSENTIAL CONCEPTS

1. Conversion disorder and somatization disorder are two major categories of somatoform disorders.

2. In conversion disorders, muscular or sensory functions are impaired with no apparent physical basis so that the symptoms seem to be linked to psychological factors.

3. It is difficult to distinguish between conversion disorder, physical illness, and malingering.

4. Somatization disorder is characterized by recurrent, multiple somatic complaints for which medical attention is sought but which have no apparent physical basis.

5. Conversion disorders occupy a historic place in psychoanalytic thinking because their nature led Freud to emphasize the unconscious. Psychoanalysis developed as a technique to overcome these repressed impulses.

6. Behaviorists suggest that conversions are reinforced and treatment focuses on teaching more effective ways to get reinforcers.

7. The dissociative disorders (dissociative amnesia, dissociative fugue, depersonalization, and dissociative identity disorder) involve disruptions of consciousness, memory, and identity.

8. The memory losses in dissociative disorders strongly suggest psychoanalytic concepts of repression. Thus, psychoanalytic techniques are widely used in treating these disorders.

KEY TERMS

Somatoform disorders (p. 160)

Dissociative disorders (p. 160)

Pain disorder (p. 160)

Body dysmorphic disorder (p. 160)

Hypochondriasis (p. 161)

Conversion disorder (p. 161)

Anesthesias (p. 162)

Hysteria (p. 162)

Malingering (p. 163)

La belle indifference (p. 163)

Factitious disorder (p. 163)

Somatization disorder (p. 163)

Dissociative amnesia (p. 171)

Dissociative fugue (p. 172)

Depersonalization disorder (p. 172)

Dissociative identity disorder [DID] (p. 172)

◆ STUDY QUESTIONS

SOMATOFORM DISORDERS (p. 160–171)

1. What are the general characteristics of somatoform disorders? Describe and distinguish among three types of somatoform disorders. (These are not discussed in detail.) (p. 160–161)

2. Give some examples of conversion symptoms involving loss of (a) muscular, and (b) sensory functioning. Why is it difficult, but important, to distinguish between conversions and medical conditions? (p. 161–163)

3. Describe somatization disorder. How is it similar to and different from conversion disorder? List several proposed causes of somatization disorder. (p. 163–165)

4. How did the study of conversions lead Freud to important concepts? Summarize Freud's early theory of conversions and his later revision of it. (p. 165–166)

5. Summarize contemporary psychodynamic research on conversions and the resulting revision of Freud's theory. (p. 166–168)

6. Describe three other approaches to conversion disorders. How well is each supported by research? (p. 168–169)

7. Why has little research been done on the psychological treatment of somatoform disorders? Summarize current treatment of somatoform disorders in terms of managing (a) anxiety and depression, (b) medical complaints, and (c) giving up symptoms. (p. 169–171)

DISSOCIATIVE DISORDERS (p. 171–180)

8. Define and distinguish among four dissociative disorders. Explain how controversy about dissociative identity disorder has been influenced by (a) changes in prevalence, (b) confusion with schizophrenia, and (c) popular cases. (p. 171–175)

9. Explain the general view of the mechanism underlying dissociative disorders. Describe two major theories of the cause of DID and a study supporting each. (p. 175–179)

10. Summarize general principles and goals for treating dissociative disorders in general and dissociative identity disorder in particular. (p. 179–180)

◆ SELF-TEST, CHAPTER 7

(* Items not covered in Study Questions.)

MULTIPLE-CHOICE

*1. Somatoform and dissociative disorders are similar in that both
  a. have symptoms suggesting a physical dysfunction.
  b. typically begin after a stressful experience.
  c. involve disruptions of consciousness.
  d. are delusional in quality.

2. Jaclyn is preoccupied with her eyes, feeling that they are asymmetrical. She spends hours applying makeup in an effort to make her eyes appear exactly the same size and shape. The extent of her routine has cost her several jobs. She has had plastic surgery, but this has not alleviated her concerns. The most likely diagnosis for Jaclyn would be
  a. body dysmorphic disorder.
  b. conversion disorder.
  c. hypochondriasis.
  d. somatization disorder.

3. The onset of conversion symptoms is usually
  a. sudden and related to a stressful situation.
  b. gradual and subtle.
  c. accompanied by great psychological distress.
  d. preceded by a period of physical illness.

*4. Tony has four major pain symptoms, namely headache, lower back pain, a knee injury, and tinnitus. He complains of ulcers and frequent diarrhea, and although there is no neurological basis, experiences numbness and tingling in his hands. Which of the following additional symptoms would confirm a diagnosis of somatization disorder?
  a. erectile dysfunction
  b. a preoccupation with a bodily feature
  c. obsessions
  d. panic attacks

5. The performance of a hysterically blind person on a visual test appears to depend on
  a. their motivation to maintain their symptom.
  b. the degree of physical impairment.
  c. the neurological basis for their symptom.
  d. their unconscious need to please the experimenter.

6. If the behavioral view of conversion disorder were accurate, then what would be true regarding experimental research on visual perception among the hysterically blind?
  a. They would accurately perceive images shown below conscious awareness.
  b. They would not be able to accurately respond to images presented to them.
  c. They would also exhibit other symptoms that would impair other cognitive processes.
  d. They would begin to show difficulties in other sensory modalities.

7. Among the dissociative disorders, dissociative fugue is characterized by
  a. massive repression.
  b. moving away and establishing a new identity.
  c. sudden development following severe stress.
  d. memory loss for virtually all past events.

8. The categorization of depersonalization as a dissociative disorder is controversial because
   a. there are no somatic symptoms.
   b. there is no associated anxiety.
   c. there is no disturbance in memory.
   d. there is a heightened sensory awareness.

9. According to one current theory, dissociative identity disorder develops in people who were ____ as children.
   a. abused
   b. overindulged
   c. unloved
   d. made to feel guilty

*10. Whereas the DSM is currently symptom-based for rendering diagnoses, the classification of dissociative identity disorder shows that diagnosis may be
   a. based on function.
   b. dimensional.
   c. theory driven.
   d. based upon personality traits.

SHORT ANSWER

1. What are the characteristics of hypochondriasis?

2. Distinguish between conversion disorder and somatization disorder.

3. How did the study of conversions lead Freud to important concepts?

4. Describe the psychodynamic studies that led to a contemporary revision of Freud's theory of conversions.

5. Summarize a behavioral account of the cause of conversion disorders.

6. How important are genetic and physiological factors in conversion disorders?

7. Why has little research been done on the psychological treatment of somatoform disorders?

8. Give several reasons the existence of dissociative identity disorder is disputed.

9. Dissociative disorders (more than other disorders) are commonly treated by psychoanalytic methods because . . .

10. What is the basic approach to treatment of dissociative disorders in general (not DID in particular)?

◆ ANSWERS TO SELF-TEST, CHAPTER 7

MULTIPLE-CHOICE

1. b (p. 160)
2. a (p. 161)
3. a (p. 162)
4. a (p. 164)
5. a (p. 166)
6. b (p. 168)
7. b (p. 172)
8. c (p. 172)
9. a (p. 175)
10. a (p. 173)

SHORT ANSWER

1. Preoccupation with fear of having a serious medical illness. (p. 161)

2. Conversion symptoms emphasize a loss of functioning while somatization disorder symptoms emphasize complaints about loss of functioning. The distinction can be hard, in practice. (p. 164)

3. Their existence led him to emphasize the unconscious. If medical causes and deliberate faking are ruled out, then the cause "must" be unconscious. (p. 165)

4. Case studies in which individuals with conversions involving blindness would "guess" visual stimuli much better or worse than chance. (p. 166)

5. The behaviors are learned. The individual may have learned (through modeling) that sick people behave this way or the behaviors may be reinforced by attention and getting out of things. (p. 168)

6. Not very important. Genetic twin research has yielded negative results (though right-brain, left-brain research suggests interesting speculations). (p. 169)

7. These people resist the idea that psychological approaches could help what they view as physical problems. Thus they are rarely available for study (p. 169)

8. The rate of DID diagnoses has varied widely depending, seemingly, on popular writings. DID was an issue in several highly publicized trials. (p. 174)

9. Psychoanalytic concepts such as unconscious and repression clearly seem applicable. (p. 179)

10. Generally treat using psychoanalytic principles and/or same approach as PTSD. (p. 179)

Chapter 8

Psychophysiological Disorders and Health Psychology

◆ OVERVIEW

The last two chapters covered psychological disorders linked to anxiety. Chapters 8 and 9 cover problems related to anxiety in more complex ways. The disorders covered in Chapters 6 and 7 were, traditionally, referred to as neuroses. Those in Chapter 6 involved more-or-less direct difficulties with anxiety. In Chapter 7 the disorders did not directly involve anxiety but, traditionally, anxiety is believed to underlie them. They were somatoform disorders (involving physical symptoms) and dissociative disorders (involving memory, consciousness, and identity). All the problems in Chapter 7 involve physical complaints without physically detectable changes in the body. In contrast, physically detectable changes are involved in the problems covered in Chapter 8.

It should be clear by now that anxiety is a source of much psychological suffering. Anxiety and stress also have physical effects. Some of these, such as heart disease, ulcers, and asthma, have traditionally been termed psychophysiological disorders. However, that term has been discarded with the realization that stress is a factor in illness and health generally. Chapter 8 discusses stress and health generally as well as the psychophysiological disorders.

Chapter 9 will cover eating disorders such as anorexia nervosa. Eating disorders also involve physical problems and tissue change. They surely result from anxiety and stress, broadly defined. However, more specifically, they appear related to cultural pressures to control weight, especially among women.

After Chapter 9, the text shifts focus. Chapters 10 and 11 cover mood disorders (such as depression) and schizophrenia. These are more complex problems, at least in terms of treatment and research (especially physiological research).

CHAPTER SUMMARY

Chapter 8 focuses on the role of psychological factors in physical illnesses generally. Psychological factors have been considered especially strong in medical conditions traditionally referred to as psychophysiological disorders. However, DSM dropped that term recognizing that psychological factors contribute to some degree to virtually all medical illnesses. The chapter discusses some common examples of psychophysiological disorders in detail.

Stress and Health reviews efforts to define and measure stress and its relation to physical illness in general. *Theories of the Stress-Illness Link* identifies a number of both biological and psychological theories regarding this relationship.

Cardiovascular Disorders including hypertension and heart disease appear related to specific styles of responding to stress, especially Type A behavior and cynicism/anger.

Asthma attacks involving difficulty in breathing result from combinations of psychological factors and biological predispositions that vary from individual to individual.

AIDS: [is] *A Challenge for the Behavioral Sciences* because behaviors and behavioral issues are central to its spread and to its control. With no medical cure yet available, efforts such as safe-sex education offer the best current hope of controlling the epidemic.

Socioeconomic Status, Ethnicity, and Health discusses socioeconomic and ethnic differences in health and longevity. While genetic factors cannot be ruled out, differences are largely related to such factors as access to care, life styles, and social stress.

Therapies for Psychophysiological Disorders involve treating current symptoms and underlying conditions using both medical and psychological approaches. Psychological approaches are used to reduce risk factors, to change general psychological contributors, and to teach specific skills. Behavioral medicine, a new specialization, is developing specialized psychological techniques to treat psychophysiological disorders and other medical conditions.

ESSENTIAL CONCEPTS

1. Psychophysiological disorders are distinct from conversion reactions and involve physical tissue changes that are caused or worsened by emotional factors.

2. There is no listing of psychophysiological disorders in DSM-IV because virtually all physical illnesses are now viewed as potentially related to psychological factors.

3. Stress has been defined in various ways, including stressful events, stress responses, and coping skills.

4. A number of research approaches indicate relationships between stress and illness. Coping skills and social supports influence these relationships.

5. There are both biological and psychological theories about the link between stress and illness.

6. There is much research on psychological factors contributing to cardiovascular disorders and asthma.

7. High blood pressure and coronary heart disease appear related to Type A behaviors, especially the suppression of anger, although this research is complex and ongoing.

8. Asthma apparently results from a combination of physical and psychological factors whose importance varies with the individual.

9. AIDS is a challenge for the behavioral sciences because, without a medical cure, psychological approaches offer the best hope of controlling the epidemic through education, etc.

10. Health and longevity vary among various socioeconomic and ethnic groups. These differences appear, at least largely, to be the result of differing access to services, lifestyles, stresses, and similar factors.

11. Where psychological factors contribute to illness, a combination of medical and psychological treatment is needed.

12. Behavioral medicine is developing specific programs for treating psychological factors that contribute to illness.

KEY TERMS

Psychophysiological disorders (p. 183)

Psychosomatic disorders (p. 183)

Psychological factors affecting a medical condition (p. 183)

Behavioral medicine (p. 183)

Health psychology (p. 183)

General adaptation syndrome [GAS] (p. 184)

Stress (p. 184)

Stressor (p. 184)

Coping (p. 185)

Structural social support (p. 190)

Functional social support (p. 190)

Somatic-weakness theory (p. 191)

Specific reaction theory (p. 191)

Anger-in theory (p. 193)

Cardiovascular disorders (p. 193)

Essential hypertension (p. 195)

Coronary heart disease [CHD] (p. 198)

Angina pectoris (p. 198)

Myocardial infarction (p. 198)

Type A behavior pattern (p. 198)

Asthma (p. 201)

Biofeedback (p. 211)

Community psychology (p. 212)

Stress management (p. 213)

◆ STUDY QUESTIONS

1. Define psychophysiological disorders, distinguishing them from conversion disorders (in Chapter 7). How does DSM-IV handle psychophysiological disorders? How does this approach lead to broader understandings of the relationship between stress and illness? (p. 183–184)

STRESS AND HEALTH (p. 184–190)

2. Describe three approaches to defining stress and the limitations of each. (p. 184–185)

3. Describe two efforts to measure stress. The first study uses a retrospective approach. Why is this approach problematic and how is the second study an improvement? Describe how coping is commonly assessed. (p. 185–190)

4. Describe two social moderators of stress. How do they influence the relationship between stress and illness? (p. 190)

THEORIES OF THE STRESS-ILLNESS LINK (p. 190–193)

5. What kinds of questions are confronted by theories of the stress-illness link? Briefly describe two reasons to be cautious about all these theories. Describe four biological theories and two psychological theories. (p. 190–193)

CARDIOVASCULAR DISORDERS (p. 193–200)

6. What is essential hypertension and how much of a problem is it? Describe the methods and results of (a) two ways of studying the relation between psychological stress and blood pressure increases, and (b) two predisposing factors in chronic increases or hypertension. (p. 195–198)

7. Describe two principal forms of coronary heart disease (CHD). Identify some traditional physical and psychological risk factors for CHD. (p. 198)

8. What limitation of traditional risk factors led to a search for diatheses to CHD? Describe Type A behavior as a possible psychological diathesis and three psychological factors that emerged from more recent research. Describe two possible biological diatheses. (p. 198–200)

ASTHMA (p. 200–204)

9. What happens in an asthma attack? Regarding the etiology of asthma, what question has been a topic of debate and what has research found? Summarize research on psychological, family, and physiological predispositions to asthma. (p. 200–204)

AIDS: A CHALLENGE FOR THE BEHAVIORAL SCIENCES (p. 204–208)

10. Why is AIDS an appropriate topic in an abnormal psychology textbook? Briefly describe the scope of the problem, description of the disease, and how it spreads. Describe efforts to prevent the spread of AIDS and their success. Identify five reasons why knowledge about AIDS may not be sufficient to prevent its spread. (p. 204–208)

SOCIOECONOMIC STATUS, ETHNICITY, AND HEALTH (p. 208–209)

11. Illustrate the role of socioeconomic status and ethnicity on health generally. What kinds of psychological factors may underlie these differences? (p. 208–209)

THERAPIES FOR PSYCHOPHYSIOLOGICAL DISORDERS (p. 209–217)

12. Why are both medical and psychological interventions needed in treating psychophysiological disorders? Describe more specific programs in five areas: (a) hypertension (methods aimed at: risk factors, exercise, relaxation, and cognitions), (b) biofeedback, (c) Type A behavior, (d) stress management, and (e) pain management (acute and chronic). (p. 209–217)

◆ SELF-TEST, CHAPTER 8

(* Items not covered in Study Questions.)

MULTIPLE-CHOICE

1. Which of the following views was fostered when DSM began requiring diagnostic judgments of psychological factors affecting medical conditions?
   a. Certain physical problems are caused by psychological stress.
   b. Certain psychological problems are caused by physical stress.
   c. All medical problems may result, in part, from psychological factors.
   d. All psychological problems may result, in part, from medical factors.

2. The most effective type of coping has been found to be
   a. inward-focused coping.
   b. problem-focused coping.
   c. emotion-focused coping.
   d. None of the above is always most effective; it depends on the situation.

3. A problem with studies on the link between psychological factors and physical health has been
   a. a general inability of respondents to report physical problems.
   b. overreporting of physical illness among individuals with high neuroticism.
   c. underreporting of physical illness among individuals with high psychoticism.
   d. the nonuniform nature of physical illness and associated psychological distress.

*4. Which of the following would be an explanation for the similarities in mortality rates between men and women currently, compared to the beginning of the twentieth century?
   a. More deaths are now due to infection and epidemics.
   b. Women smoke and drink less than men.
   c. Most deaths result from diseases that are affected by lifestyle, and lifestyle differences between men and women are decreasing.
   d. Men are more preoccupied with their health now.

5. Which of the following is *not* a predisposing factor in hypertension?
   a. social isolation
   b. getting angry easily
   c. sensitivity to salt
   d. sedentary lifestyle

6. In the Western Collaborative Group Study, after traditional risk factors were controlled for, Type A subjects
   a. were twice as likely to develop coronary heart disease (CHD) as other subjects.
   b. had only a slightly increased risk for developing CHD.
   c. were actually *less* likely to develop CHD than other subjects.
   d. were more likely to develop CHD only if they also had a parental history of heart attacks.

7. The newly proposed Type D personality
   a. is closely associated with emotional expression.
   b. has been defined as negative affect in conjunction with inhibition in expression.
   c. has been shown to be a protective factor from coronary heart disease.
   d. is similar to Type A personality, but is less severe.

8. Regardless of original etiology of asthma, asthma sufferers report that most attacks
   a. can be controlled.
   b. are precipitated by anxiety.
   c. follow physical exertion.
   d. are preceded by an aura.

9. Recent efforts aimed at reducing the number of AIDS infections have
   a. focused upon religious practices.
   b. included social skills training to increase sexual assertiveness skills.
   c. focused upon specific at-risk groups.
   d. largely relied upon condom-distribution.

10. Biofeedback is
   a. a technique used to train people to control otherwise involuntary physical activity.
   b. generally ineffective in treating essential hypertension.
   c. useful in focusing attention on the physical problems.
   d. equivalent to a placebo.

SHORT ANSWER

1. Psychophysiological disorders are not a category in DSM-IV because . . .

2. Why was it difficult to apply Selye's theory of stress to psychology?

3. Define "functional social support."

4. Summarize the somatic-weakness theory.

5. How does psychoanalysis account for the fact that people develop different psychophysiological disorders when exposed to the (apparently) same stressors?

6. How important a health problem is essential hypertension?

7. According to research, blood pressure increases in individuals who respond to chronic stress by . . . (doing what?)

8. What do people experience when they have an asthma attack?

9. What is the most important reason for ethnic and racial differences in overall health and longevity?

10. Describe the treatment for Type A behavior.

◆ ANSWERS TO SELF-TEST, CHAPTER 8

MULTIPLE-CHOICE

1. c (p. 183)	2. d (p. 185)	3. b (p. 191)	4. c (p. 194)
5. d (p. 196–197)	6. a (p. 199)	7. b (p. 200)	8. b (p. 203)
9. b (p. 206)	10. a (p. 211)		

SHORT ANSWER

1. Virtually all physical diseases are recognized as potentially related to psychological stress. (p. 183)

2. It was not clear how stress should be defined: in terms of stimuli, responses, or individual differences in ability to cope. (p. 184–185)

3. The quality of an individual's friendships: having close friends that can be called on in time of need. (p. 190)

4. Disorders will appear in whichever physical system is weakest or most vulnerable to stress. (p. 191)

5. Unconscious, unresolved conflicts influence how individuals respond to stress thus producing different disorders. (p. 193)

6. Called the "silent killer" (because people aren't aware of and don't check their blood pressure), essential hypertension is the cause of 90% of cases of high blood pressure which contributes to many medical problems. (p. 195)

7. Holding their anger in. Not responding. Remaining angry and resentful. (p. 196)

8. Sudden onset with tightness in chest, wheezing, coughing. Increased fluid in lungs, eyes, etc. Fear of suffocation. (p. 200)

9. Most important reason is lifestyle and socioeconomic differences such as access to health care. (Biological factors are of some importance in some illnesses but less important overall.) (p. 208)

10. Multifaceted programs encourage more relaxed behaviors (talk slower, listen more), reduce anger and stress from TV and work, cognitive changes to stop seeing everything as a challenge that must be met, etc. (p. 213)

Chapter 9

Eating Disorders

◆ OVERVIEW

This is the last of four chapters covering topics related to anxiety and stress. The previous chapters included Chapters 6 and 7 discussing psychological disorders related to anxiety and stress in various ways. Chapter 8 discussed effects of anxiety and stress on medical illnesses and on the body generally. We have long recognized stress's contribution to the psychophysiological disorders (such as ulcers); however, that term has been dropped with recognition that stress can play a role in virtually all physical problems.

Chapter 9 turns to another set of disorders, eating disorders, which also involve physical effects of anxiety and stress. Eating disorders, such as anorexia nervosa, involve physical changes severe enough to be fatal. They certainly involve anxiety and stress. However, in this case, the anxiety and stress seem to result from cultural pressures on people, especially young women, to control their weight.

After Chapter 9, the text shifts to two disorders that are more complex. They are mood disorders such as depression (Chapter 10), and schizophrenia (Chapter 11). Both have been widely studied and, for various reasons, much of the research has focused on genetic and physiological issues.

CHAPTER SUMMARY

Clinical Description of three disorders is provided. Anorexia nervosa involves inadequate food intake so that the victim, usually female, may starve to death. Bulimia, in which individuals gorge themselves then purge the food by vomiting or using laxatives, is less life-threatening but can also have serious physical consequences. Binge eating disorder (a proposed diagnosis for further study in DSM-IV) describes individuals who experience recurrent eating binges without purging or weight loss (indeed, commonly with weight gain or fluctuation). Binge eating disorder is not well understood and is not discussed further.

Etiology of Eating Disorders appears to be complex and variable. Biological factors have been hypothesized based on genetic data and knowledge of brain mechanisms in eating. Sociocultural factors are strongly suggested by correlations between eating disorders and social pressure to be thin as reflected in advertising, etc. Other views have focused on childhood, personality, and family or abuse issues. Cognitive-behavioral views emphasize irrational beliefs about the necessity of being thin and about controlling eating in order to be acceptable.

Treatment of Eating Disorders describes problems in treating these complex conditions. Biological treatment using antidepressants has yielded mixed results. Anorexics can be kept alive by hospitalizing them to maintain their weight. Treatment of issues underlying anorexia and bulimia has been more difficult, with various methods to address the potential combination of family, social, and psychological factors.

ESSENTIAL CONCEPTS

1. Two long-recognized eating disorders are anorexia nervosa (in which people do not eat) and bulimia nervosa (in which people have eating binges followed by purging).

2. Binge eating disorder, describing individuals who have eating binges without purging, is proposed in DSM-IV as a new diagnosis for further study.

3. Eating disorders may have a genetic liability although adoption studies are needed. Brain chemicals involved in controlling normal appetite may be disrupted in eating-disordered individuals.

4. Social pressures especially on women to be thin, to diet, etc. appear to be significant factors leading to eating disorders.

5. Dynamic views stress developmental factors so that extreme thinness becomes a side effect of establishing independence. Family systems views propose that eating problems allow the family to ignore larger conflicts. Personality and family data are difficult to interpret but lend some support.

6. Cognitive-behavioral views suggest that these individuals have unrealistic beliefs about the necessity of being thin and/or poor skills in moderating their eating.

7. Antidepressants have shown some success in treating bulimia although dropout rates are high.

8. Anorexics may require hospitalization to manage medical complications. Providing social reinforcers for eating and weight gain has been somewhat successful. Treatment focuses on challenging beliefs about being thin and on building normal eating behaviors. Treatment of underlying issues (and long-term weight maintenance) is difficult.

KEY TERMS

Anorexia nervosa (p. 222)

Bulimia nervosa (p. 225)

Binge eating disorder (p. 226)

◆ STUDY QUESTIONS

CLINICAL DESCRIPTION (p. 222–226)

1. Three diagnostic labels are identified. For each label summarize the (a) distinguishing features, (b) subtypes, (c) relationship to other psychological problems, (d) physical effects, and (e) prognosis. (Note that binge eating disorder is a tentative label and not yet well understood.) (p. 222–226)

ETIOLOGY OF EATING DISORDERS (p. 226–236)

2. Under biological factors, what data suggests a genetic contribution to eating disorders? Describe how three areas of brain research may be related to eating disorders. (p. 226–227)

3. Briefly describe studies of social influences on eating disorders in four areas (sociocultural variables in industrialized countries, gender influences, cross-cultural studies, and racial differences). (p. 227–229)

4. Summarize the basis of eating disorders according to Bruch's psychodynamic view and Minuchin's family systems view. Summarize what has been found about the personalities, the families, and the backgrounds of individuals with eating disorders. (p. 231–234)

5. Summarize the cognitive-behavioral view of anorexia nervosa and of bulimia nervosa. (p. 234–236)

TREATMENT OF EATING DISORDERS (p. 236–239)

6. Summarize the effectiveness of biological treatment of bulimia (including two problems) and of anorexia. (p. 236)

7. Describe the goals, methods, and effectiveness of two stages in treating anorexia. Describe Minuchin's family therapy approach to the second stage. (p. 236–237)

8. Describe a cognitive behavioral approach to treatment of bulimia. Include description of both behavioral methods (to alter actual eating) and cognitive methods (to alter beliefs). (p. 237–238)

◆ SELF-TEST, CHAPTER 9

(* Items not covered in Study Questions.)

MULTIPLE-CHOICE

1. Individuals with anorexia nervosa
   a. stop eating because of an abnormal increase in blood sugar, which alters their perceptions of hunger.
   b. fear gaining weight so much that they stop eating.
   c. have lost their appetite, leading them to stop eating.
   d. stop eating but do not lose weight.

2. Distorted body image in anorexics is often manifested by
   a. extreme avoidance of mirrors and scales.
   b. critical evaluation of body areas such as stomach and buttocks.
   c. frequent questioning of others regarding their appearance.
   d. checking behaviors designed to ensure that their stomach and buttocks appear smaller than in reality.

3. What is the most likely prognosis for a person with anorexia nervosa?
   a. regain normal weight as they enter puberty
   b. develop bulimia nervosa
   c. enter treatment and maintain normal weight following treatment
   d. continue to struggle with the disorder whether or not they get treatment

4. Compared to the binge, purging is felt by many bulimics to be
   a. a source of relief.
   b. more anxiety producing.
   c. more disgusting.
   d. a source of pride.

5. Which brain structure has been hypothesized to play a role in eating disorders?
   a. frontal lobe
   b. hippocampus
   c. hypothalamus
   d. pituitary gland

6. The incidence of eating disorders has been rising steadily since the 1950s. This provides the best evidence for the ___________ theory of eating disorder.
   a. biological
   b. sociocultural
   c. psychodynamic
   d. family systems

7. Studies of the personality of anorexics indicate that they are generally
   a. impulsive, adventurous, outgoing.
   b. confused, disoriented, withdrawn.
   c. shy, obedient, perfectionistic.
   d. warm, sensitive, helpful.

8. In the cognitive-behavioral view, the non-eating of anorexics is reinforced by
   a. reducing anxiety about being fat.
   b. reducing sexual demands from males.
   c. attention of overly concerned family members.
   d. increased time and energy for studies.

9. The first step in treating anorexia nervosa is
   a. medication to reduce anxiety about eating.
   b. education on the importance of a well balanced diet.
   c. hospitalization to promote and monitor eating.
   d. assessment to identify causes and plan individualized treatment.

10. The ultimate goal of Minuchin's family lunch session in treating anorexia is to get the parents to
   a. take responsibility for their role in the problem.
   b. cooperate in working with their daughter.
   c. force their daughter to eat.
   d. quit trying to force their daughter to eat.

SHORT ANSWER

1. What are some physical effects of bulimia nervosa purging type?

2. What are several characteristics of bulimic women in addition to eating patterns?

3. Is there a genetic diathesis for eating disorders? Explain.

4. How do cross-cultural data indicate the role of social/cultural factors in eating disorders?

5. Summarize Bruch's psychodynamic view of eating disorders.

6. What has research shown about the families of individuals with eating disorders?

7. How is the cognitive-behavioral view of bulimia different from its view of anorexia?

8. Describe the effectiveness of biological treatments for eating disorders.

9. Describe cognitive methods to alter the beliefs of bulimics.

10. Describe cognitive-behavioral methods to alter the actual eating behavior of bulimics.

◆ ANSWERS TO SELF-TEST, CHAPTER 9

MULTIPLE-CHOICE

1. b (p. 222)	2. b (p. 223)	3. d (p. 224)	4. a (p. 225)
5. c (p. 226)	6. b (p. 227–228)	7. c (p. 232)	8. a (p. 234–235)
9. c (p. 236)	10. b (p. 237)		

SHORT ANSWER

1. Frequent purging can change electrolyte balances, produce tooth decay from stomach acid, salivary glands can become swollen, inhaled food particles can cause lung infections, etc. (p. 226)

2. Depression, anxiety, personality disorders. Problems with stealing and promiscuity suggest impulsiveness. (p. 225–226)

3. Eating disorders four times more likely in close relatives. Higher concordance in MZ than DZ twins. These suggest a genetic diathesis — although adoptee studies have not been done. (p. 226)

4. Eating disorders (and social emphasis on thinness) appear more prevalent in industrialized countries, although evidence is skimpy. (p. 229)

5. Children raised feeling ineffectual by parents who impose wishes on child ignoring child's desires. Child does not learn to recognize internal needs (like hunger) and seizes on societal emphasis on thinness as way to be in control and have an identity. (p. 231)

6. Confusing studies. Patients report family conflict, but not parents. Some evidence of disturbed relations but don't fit theories and unclear as based on reports, not observations. (p. 232–234)

7. Bulimics are assumed to be similar to anorexics except they have more rigid self-rules and/or less self-control over eating. After binges, purging reduces their anxiety but lowers self-esteem so the cycle repeats. (p. 235)

8. Drugs have not proven effective in anorexia. Depressed bulimics are helped by antidepressants although many drop out and effects last only as long as drug is taken. (p. 236)

9. Urged to identify, question, and change beliefs that weight is vital to acceptance by self and others, that only extreme dieting can control weight. (p. 237–238)

10. Client brings "forbidden" food to session and eats with relaxation and coaching to not purge. Discuss thoughts and feelings while actually eating. Urged to eat normal well-balanced meals. (p. 238)

Chapter 10

Mood Disorders

◆ OVERVIEW

The previous four chapters covered a wide range of problems related, in one way or another, to anxiety and stress. They included both psychological disorders and medical conditions in which anxiety and stress are prominent.

The text now discusses two groups of disorders in which physiological factors have been widely studied. They are mood disorders, such as depression, and schizophrenia. Complex, and similar, physiological theories involving neurotransmitters (colloquially, brain imbalances) have been developed for both disorders.

Chapter 10 covers mood disorders, including lowered mood (depression) and heightened mood (mania). Chapter 10 also discusses suicide, which is often associated with depression. The literature on mood disorders is complex. Physiological and genetic factors have long been studied, both because drugs are effective in treating them and because manic individuals experience rapid mood shifts that often seem, otherwise, inexplicable. Psychological research has also been extensive and psychological therapies have proven effective.

For similar reasons, physiological and genetic factors have long been suspected in schizophrenia (Chapter 11). Schizophrenia has been the subject of extensive research. It has been a difficult problem to understand and to treat. Drugs are a core part of treatment but are only partially effective.

After Chapters 10 and 11, the text shifts to disorders in which social and behavioral issues seem more prominent.

CHAPTER SUMMARY

The chapter begins by describing *General Characteristics of Mood Disorders.* DSM labels are based on the pattern and severity of depressive and manic episodes. Individuals with very different or heterogeneous behaviors receive the same label, suggesting other distinctions may be important.

Psychological Theories of Mood Disorders are well developed and varied. Psychoanalytic theory suggests that dependent people remain stuck in sadness because they cannot work through the anger that all people experience following a loss. Beck's cognitive theory suggests that depressives understand events through cognitive distortions that lead them to blame themselves for negative outcomes. Helplessness/hopelessness theory suggests that difficulty controlling negative events leads people to attribute the difficulty to themselves and feel hopeless about influencing outcomes — resulting in depression. An interpersonal approach suggests depressed individuals have fewer social supports, perhaps because their ineffective behaviors lead others to avoid them. Theories of mania are less well developed but view mania as a defense against depressing ideas about self.

Biological Theories of Mood Disorders seem important because of a genetic predisposition, especially for bipolar disorders. Research indicates that depressives and manics have difficulty with certain brain neurotransmitters; however, the nature of this difficulty is unclear. Neuroendocrine difficulties are also suggested.

Therapies for Mood Disorders include psychotherapeutic approaches derived from psychological theories of depression as well as somatic treatments including electroconvulsive shock and drugs. Considerable research has studied the relative effectiveness and utility of these approaches.

Depression in Childhood and Adolescence is relatively (but not totally) similar to adult depression. Treatment is largely psychological and based on the special needs of children.

Suicide is partially related to depression although many suicidal individuals are not obviously depressed or otherwise disordered. The text reviews basic facts and theories, describes approaches to preventing suicide, and discusses ethical issues in dealing with suicide.

ESSENTIAL CONCEPTS

1. DSM-IV lists two major mood disorders (major depression and bipolar disorder) and two chronic mood disorders (dysthymic and cyclothymic disorder).

2. Freud proposed that orally fixated people who experience a loss are unable to accept the anger that results so that they do not stop grieving and become depressed.

3. Beck suggests that depression results from cognitive schemata involving negative views of the self, the world, and the future.

4. The learned helplessness theory of depression evolved out of research that found depressive-like behaviors in animals exposed to inescapable aversive events. The current version emphasizes feelings of hopelessness that result from self-blame for aversive events.

5. Interpersonal approaches note that depressed people have fewer social supports, perhaps because their behaviors lead others to avoid them.

6. There is little psychological theorizing regarding bipolar disorder. Generally mania is seen as a defense against depression or similar states.

7. Genetic data indicate there is a heritable component to major mood disorders, especially bipolar disorder.

8. Biological theories developed out of drug research and suggest problems with certain neurotransmitters or with hormones secreted in the brain.

9. Physiological and psychological theories of depression are probably two different ways to describe the same phenomenon.

10. Beck's cognitive therapy has been widely studied for treating depression.

11. There are a number of biological treatments for depression including electroconvulsive therapy and antidepressant drugs. Lithium is a useful drug in treating bipolar disorder. Some approaches can have serious side effects.

12. Depressed children are similar to depressed adults (but more suicide, guilt, etc.). Psychological treatments are effective.

13. While all people who commit suicide are not depressed, many people who are depressed think about or attempt taking their own life.

14. Suicide prevention centers have developed methods to help people who are considering suicide.

15. Traditionally therapists have devoted themselves to preventing suicide although this can raise quality-of-life issues. More recent debates over physician-assisted suicide raise additional issues.

To My Students

This chapter covers both depression and the related topic of suicide. Estimates are that 20 percent of students will consider suicide during college. You might consider what you would do if a friend (or you) feels suicidal. You will find some ideas in the chapter. However, you would also want to seek professional help. Most areas of the United States have 24-hour crisis telephone lines. Get the telephone number for the crisis line in your area (and in your home town if you're living away from home). Write it in your appointment book or some other handy spot. You can probably get the number from your instructor, college counseling center, or the local mental health clinic. Sometimes this is "911" but some 911 centers will refer you to another number.

KEY TERMS

Mood disorders (p. 241)

Depression (p. 241)

Mania (p. 241)

Major [or unipolar] depression (p. 242)

Bipolar I disorder (p. 243)

Hypomania (p. 244)

Cyclothymic disorder (p. 245)

Dysthymic disorder (p. 245)

Logotherapy (p. 247)

Negative triad (p. 247)

Learned helplessness theory (p. 249)

Attribution (p. 250)

Tricyclic drugs (p. 254)

Monoamine oxidase inhibitors (p. 254)

Electroconvulsive therapy [ECT] (p. 264)

Bilateral ECT (p. 264)

Unilateral ECT (p. 264)

Lithium carbonate (p. 265)

Egoistic suicide (p. 273)

Altruistic suicide (p. 273)

Anomic suicide (p. 273)

Suicide prevention centers (p. 276)

◆ STUDY QUESTIONS

GENERAL CHARACTERISTICS OF MOOD DISORDERS (p. 241–246)

1. Give at least five different general characteristics of depression and of mania. (p. 241–242) Distinguish among the two major mood disorders (p. 242–244) and the two chronic mood disorders (p. 245–246) in DSM-IV. What is meant by heterogeneity within the categories? (p. 244–245)

PSYCHOLOGICAL THEORIES OF MOOD DISORDERS (p. 246–253)

2. Describe the psychoanalytic theory of (normal) bereavement. What childhood circumstances may cause bereavement to go astray and how? What is the current status of this theory? (p. 246)

3. Describe the three levels of cognitive activity that lead to depressed feelings according to Beck. Evaluate this theory by describing research on two points. (p. 246–249)

4. Describe three stages in the evolution of the helplessness/hopelessness theory of depression. What five problems remain? (p. 249–252)

5. Summarize an interpersonal theory of depression by describing five interpersonal characteristics of depressed individuals. According to research, do these characteristics lead to depression, result from depression, or both? (p. 252–253)

6. How have most psychological theories viewed the two phases of bipolar disorder? Describe a study suggesting that manics try to conceal low self-esteem. (p. 253)

BIOLOGICAL THEORIES OF MOOD DISORDERS (p. 253–257)

7. What three research areas (starting on p. 254 to 256) suggest biological factors in mood disorders? What has genetic research found regarding inheritance of bipolar depression? of unipolar depression? (p. 254)

8. What are the theorized roles of norepinephrine and serotonin in mania and in depression? Describe the drug actions that led to these theories. Describe two research approaches used to evaluate these theories (and the limitation of each). Describe new findings regarding drug actions and how they have an impact on the theories. (p. 254–256)

9. Which part of the neuroendocrine system has been linked to depression and how? What do the neurotransmitter and neuroendocrine findings suggest about psychological theories of depression? (p. 256–257)

THERAPIES FOR MOOD DISORDERS (p. 257–269)

10. Regarding psychological therapies for depression, briefly describe two psychodynamic therapies, cognitive/behavior therapy (p. 257), and social skills training (p. 260). Describe the NIMH research program (p. 258–260) including its importance, the groups and procedures, seven findings, and one controversy. Describe three general goals of psychological treatment for bipolar disorder. (p. 560)

11. Three biological therapies are discussed. For each describe its effectiveness, advantages, and disadvantages. (p. 264–266)

DEPRESSION IN CHILDHOOD AND ADOLESCENCE (p. 266–269)

12. Compare child or adolescent depression to adult depression regarding (a) symptoms, (b) prevalence, (c) etiology, and (d) biological and psychological therapies. (p. 266–269)

SUICIDE (p. 269–280)

13. Do nondepressed people commit suicide? Review and be able to recognize 15 facts about suicide. Summarize six ideas as perspectives on suicide. (p. 269–272)

14. Describe four theories of suicide. According to psychological tests, what are three characteristics of people likely to, or not likely to, commit suicide? List two reasons it is difficult to predict suicide in individual cases. (p. 272–275)

15. Summarize Schneidman's approach to suicide prevention and the general approach of suicide prevention centers. What clinical and ethical issues do health professionals face in preventing suicide and in assisting suicide? (p. 275–280)

◆ SELF-TEST, CHAPTER 10

(* Items not covered in Study Questions.)

MULTIPLE-CHOICE

1. Vanessa reported feeling a lack of energy, difficulty sleeping, not eating, difficulty concentrating, and a loss of interest in activities she previously enjoyed. Which of the following is the *most* likely diagnosis for Vanessa?
   a. eating disorder
   b. major depression
   c. bipolar disorder
   d. generalized anxiety disorder

2. Jack reports being in a wonderful mood. He has been very active at work lately, even working far into the night, as he seems to need only a few hours of sleep. He is very talkative and quickly moves from one topic to another, describing a scheme he has for making a fortune in the stock market. Which of the following diagnoses best fits Jack?
   a. overanxious disorder
   b. dysthymic disorder
   c. bipolar disorder
   d. None of the above; Jack does not fit the criteria for a mental disorder.

3. Iris has been feeling depressed most of the time for the past three years. She generally feels inadequate, sleeps a great deal, has trouble concentrating, and avoids social contact. The most likely diagnosis for Iris would be
   a. cyclothymic disorder.
   b. bipolar I disorder.
   c. dysthymic disorder.
   d. hypomania.

4. According to Freud's theory, a depressed person is fixated in which stage of development?
   a. oral
   b. anal
   c. genital
   d. phallic

5. Depressive cognitive biases, according to the cognitive theory of depression, are
   a. pessimistic global views of self, world, and future.
   b. negative beliefs about how things work in the world.
   c. negative schemata triggered by negative life events.
   d. distorted ways of reaching conclusions about events.

6. Which of the following is suggested by an interpersonal theory of depression?
   a. Depressive behaviors are reinforced by others seeking to cheer up the individual.
   b. Interpersonal trauma leads to withdrawal and depression.
   c. Depressed people withdraw from social contact and, over time, lose social skills.
   d. Poor social skills both lead to and result from depression.

7. Research investigating the effects of medication upon depression is recently focusing upon
   a. how side effects of the medication play a role in the reduction of depression.
   b. the effects upon the postsynaptic site during medication trials.
   c. glucose metabolism changes due to medication withdrawal.
   d. the joint effects of hormonal regulation and medication administration.

8. Adults with depression are more likely to have which of the following symptoms when compared to children with depression?
   a. suicide attempts and guilt
   b. fatigue and suicidal ideation
   c. loss of appetite and early morning depression
   d. delusions

9. Which of the following describes the relationship between depression and suicide?
   a. Almost all people who commit suicide are depressed.
   b. Almost all people who are depressed attempt suicide.
   c. Although depressed people often attempt suicide, many suicides are committed by people who are *not* depressed.
   d. Contrary to popular belief, there is no relationship between depression and suicide.

10. A businessman commits suicide when he must file for bankruptcy. According to Durkheim, this is which type of suicide?
   a. altruistic
   b. egoistic
   c. intrinsic
   d. anomic

SHORT ANSWER

1. List five characteristics of depression in addition to feeling sad.

2. How do childhood events cause adults to experience depression (rather than mourning) following a loss according to psychoanalysis?

3. Summarize the current version of the helplessness theory of depression.

4. Describe a study suggesting that manics try to conceal low self-esteem.

5. Describe two strategies used in research on the relationship between neurotransmitters and depression.

6. How is the neuroendocrine system linked to depression?

7. What do therapists do to treat depression based on cognitive theories of its cause?

8. Identify one advantage and one disadvantage to drug treatment for serious depression.

9. Why has it been difficult to develop psychological tests to predict suicide?

10. Describe Schneidman's approach to suicide prevention.

◆ ANSWERS TO SELF-TEST, CHAPTER 10

MULTIPLE-CHOICE

1. b (p. 241)
2. c (p. 241–242)
3. c (p. 245–246)
4. a (p. 246)
5. a (p. 247)
6. d (p. 252)
7. b (p. 256)
8. c (p. 266)
9. c (p. 269)
10. d (p. 273)

SHORT ANSWER

1. Change in sleep, eating, activity. Loss of interest, concentration, and energy. Social withdrawal. Negative feelings about self, thoughts of suicide. (p. 241)

2. Childhood over or undergratification leaves the person overly dependent. Thus, following a loss, they cannot be angry at the person for leaving them and turn the anger inward. (p. 246)

3. Emphasizes hopelessness. Individuals have low self-esteem and attribute negative experiences to factors which are internal, stable, global. Thus they feel hopeless. (p. 250–251)

4. Manics reported good self-esteem but showed poor self-esteem on an indirect test (inferring esteem of the character in a short story). (p. 253)

5. (a) Study metabolic byproducts of neurotransmitters in the blood, urine, etc. (b) Study whether drugs that influence neurotransmitters also influence the disorders. (p. 254–255)

6. The neuroendocrine system consists of brain areas (hypothalamus, etc.) that release hormones which influence depression-related behaviors such as appetite, sleep. Overactivity in these areas could be part of depression. (p. 256)

7. Help clients identify and change their beliefs using logical analysis, providing contrary examples or experiences, etc. (p. 257–258)

8. Advantage: they hasten recovery. Disadvantages: drug side-effects, relapse common if drug is discontinued. (p. 265)

9. Tests could not detect situational causes. Suicide is so very infrequent tests cannot predict accurately enough. (p. 257)

10. Schneidman emphasizes helping them to find and consider other alternatives (also to reduce suffering, reconsider suicide). (p. 275–276)

Chapter 11

Schizophrenia

◆ OVERVIEW

Chapters 10 and 11 discuss two disorders that have been the subject of extensive research. Similar physiological theories have developed implicating brain neurotransmitters in both disorders. Mood disorders (Chapter 10) have been the subject of extensive psychological and physiological research with effective treatments emerging from both areas. Schizophrenia (Chapter 11) has led to even more extensive study, at least in part because no overt cure exists.

Of all the disorders covered in the text, schizophrenia comes closest to the common understanding of being “crazy.” Despite extensive study, it remains a major concern both socially and scientifically. Historically, psychopathologists have disagreed on how to define schizophrenia and even on whether the term refers to one or to several different problems. Despite recent advances, no cure for schizophrenia has emerged. Currently a combination of approaches emphasizing drugs can manage, but not cure, the problem. Schizophrenics are a major portion of mental hospital and health clinic patients.

After Chapter 11, the focus of the text shifts to disorders that often seem to be more social and behavioral in nature. These include substance abuse and dependence disorders (Chapter 12), personality disorders including antisocial personality disorder (Chapter 13), and sexual and gender identity disorders (Chapter 14).

CHAPTER SUMMARY

Schizophrenia is a complex disorder and difficult to define. The *Clinical Symptoms of Schizophrenia* include positive symptoms (or behavioral excesses such as confused thinking and speaking) and negative symptoms (or behavioral deficits including lack of energy, interest, and feelings).

The *History of the Concept of Schizophrenia* has included two traditions. Many American ideas about schizophrenia developed out of Bleuler's broad, psychoanalytically based definition. Recent DSM editions have moved toward Kraepelin’s narrower, descriptive (rather than theoretical) approach, which has always been popular in Europe. Currently DSM-IV recognizes three subcategories of schizophrenia. Disorganized schizophrenics exhibit blatantly bizarre and silly behaviors. Catatonic schizophrenics show primarily motor symptoms including wild excitement and apathetic withdrawal to the point of immobility. Paranoid schizophrenics have well-organized delusions of persecution, grandiosity, and jealousy. Current research suggests the distinction between positive and negative symptoms represents another useful way to subcategorize schizophrenia.

Research on the *Etiology of Schizophrenia* has been extensive. Genetic, biochemical, and neurological data strongly suggest a biological diathesis to schizophrenia. Genetic data from family, twin, and more sophisticated adoptee studies all point to a genetic predisposition to schizophrenia. Biochemical research suggests excessive activity in nerve tracts of the brain that utilize the neurotransmitter dopamine for some schizophrenics. New neurological techniques suggest brain atrophy in schizophrenics with negative symptoms. Prenatal infections may be involved for these individuals.

Other research has looked at social class, family, and other variables. Since schizophrenia runs in families it is possible to select and follow children with a high risk of becoming schizophrenic. These studies suggest stressors that may potentiate the diatheses suggested by biological research.

Many biological and psychological *Therapies for Schizophrenia* have been attempted. Antipsychotic drugs were a major advance. However schizophrenics need additional help to cope with social living. Traditional psychotherapeutic approaches have not been very effective with schizophrenics, but family and behavioral methods show promise. There remains a need to integrate skills and knowledge of various disciplines in order to help schizophrenics lead as normal a life as possible.

ESSENTIAL CONCEPTS

1. Most symptoms of schizophrenia can be grouped into positive symptoms (or behavioral excesses such as confused thinking and speaking) and negative symptoms (or behavioral deficits including lack of energy, interest, and feelings).

2. Historic definitions of schizophrenia included Kraepelin's concept of dementia praecox and Bleuler's concept of loose associative threads. Currently DSM-IV has moved to Kraepelin's narrower definition.

3. DSM-IV defines three major subcategories of schizophrenia: disorganized, catatonic, and paranoid. These subcategories are limited. Research suggests the distinction between positive and negative symptoms may provide more useful distinctions.

4. Evidence from family, twin, and adoptee studies indicates a substantial genetic diathesis to schizophrenia, although this alone cannot fully explain the disorder's etiology.

5. Extensive research links dopamine activity in particular brain tracts to schizophrenia. The evidence suggests that both genetic and prenatal factors may lead to dopamine tract changes.

6. There is a link between low social status and schizophrenia. Sociogenic and social-selection explanations have been offered for this correlation.

7. Early theories that family issues cause schizophrenia have been discredited. However family patterns of communication and emotional expression may affect the post-hospital adjustment of schizophrenics.

8. Children of schizophrenic patients have been studied longitudinally in high-risk projects which shed light on the etiology of schizophrenia.

9. Currently no treatments of schizophrenia are totally effective. Neuroleptic medications are effective in controlling the positive symptoms of schizophrenia.

10. Family therapy and behavioral approaches show promise in improving the social adjustment of schizophrenics.

11. There remains a need to integrate skills of many disciplines to better help schizophrenics.

To My Students

Schizophrenia is a serious and complex problem. Traditional paradigms have generated a tremendous amount of research. Unfortunately no paradigm has proven highly useful and our understanding of this problem remains limited.

As a result this chapter spends little time describing paradigms and considerable time summarizing research. At times the discussion becomes unavoidably complex, especially when summarizing the genetic and physiological research. You may want to refer to the basic discussion of these topics in Chapter 2 of the text, especially pages 21 to 24.

The study questions indicate the core ideas to look for as you study. Take your time and ask your instructor if you have questions.

KEY TERMS

Schizophrenia (p. 283)

Positive symptoms (p. 283)

Disorganized speech [thought disorder] (p. 284)

Incoherence (p. 284)

Loose associations [derailment] (p. 284)

Delusions (p. 284)

Hallucinations (p. 285)

Negative symptoms (p. 286)

Avolition (p. 286)

Alogia (p. 286)

Anhedonia (p. 286)

Flat affect (p. 286)

Asociality (p. 287)

Catatonic immobility (p. 287)

Waxy flexibility (p. 287)

Inappropriate affect (p. 287)

Dementia praecox (p. 288)

Delusional disorder (p. 290)

Disorganized schizophrenia (p. 290)

Catatonic schizophrenia (p. 290)

Paranoid schizophrenia (p. 290)

Grandiose delusions (p. 290)

Delusional jealousy (p. 290)

Ideas of reference (p. 290)

Undifferentiated schizophrenia (p. 290)

Residual schizophrenia (p. 290)

Labeling theory (p. 292)

Dopamine theory (p. 295)

Sociogenic hypothesis (p. 301)

Social-selection theory (p. 301)

Schizophrenogenic mother (p. 301)

Expressed emotion [EE] (p. 302)

Prefrontal lobotomy (p. 304)

Antipsychotic drugs (p. 305)

◆ STUDY QUESTIONS

CLINICAL SYMPTOMS OF SCHIZOPHRENIA (p. 283–287)

1. Summarize the symptoms of schizophrenia including three positive symptoms and five negative symptoms plus two others. Give examples of the various terms explaining why they are positive or negative symptoms. (p. 283–287)

HISTORY OF THE CONCEPT (p. 288–291)

2. Describe Kraepelin's and Bleuler's early views on schizophrenia. Trace the way Bleuler's view broadened in America. List five ways in which the newer DSM definitions of schizophrenia have moved toward the narrower, European, view. (p. 288–290)

3. Summarize several distinguishing characteristics of each of the three subtypes of schizophrenia in DSM-IV. Evaluate these subtypes by describing (a) their limitations and (b) evolving interest in another approach to subdividing schizophrenia. (p. 290–291)

ETIOLOGY OF SCHIZOPHRENIA (p. 291–304)

4. Describe and evaluate three approaches to studying genetic factors in schizophrenia. Summarize the overall importance of genetic factors. (p. 291–295)

5. Why does genetic evidence suggest the need to study biochemical factors in schizophrenia? Summarize three findings indicating dopamine activity is a factor in schizophrenia. Summarize current views on (a) dopamine levels vs. dopamine receptors and (b) positive vs. negative symptoms. How could different neural pathways allow prefrontal underactivity to effect both negative symptoms and, indirectly, positive symptoms? Identify three weaknesses to current dopamine theory and two other chemicals that may be involved. (p. 295–298)

6. Summarize data implicating (a) enlarged ventricles and (b) the prefrontal cortex in schizophrenia. What suggests these differences are not purely genetic? Summarize data suggesting they may result from (a) birth complications or (b) viral infection before birth. (p. 298–300)

7. What is the relationship between social class and schizophrenia? (What does it mean to say this is not a "continuous progression"?) Describe two theories of this relationship and a recent Israeli study comparing them. (p. 300–301)

8. According to research, what family patterns may contribute to schizophrenia and influence the post-hospitalization adjustment of schizophrenics? What is the advantage of high-risk studies in studying the development of schizophrenia? What have high-risk studies found (especially regarding positive and negative symptoms)? (p. 301–304)

THERAPIES FOR SCHIZOPHRENIA (p. 304–315)

9. Why were earlier biological treatments abandoned? What are the benefits and the problems of antipsychotic drugs? What is current clinical practice regarding their use? How did the introduction of clozapine stimulate change? (p. 304–306)

10. The text describes three general psychological treatment approaches and three recent cognitive-behavioral approaches. For each, describe the (a) rationale, (b) method, and (c) results — if any. Summarize the origins and rationale of case management. (p. 306–312)

11. Summarize general trends in treatment in terms of the overall trend and four specific points. Identify four ongoing issues in the care of patients with schizophrenia. (p. 312–315)

◆ SELF-TEST, CHAPTER 11

(* Items not covered in Study Questions.)

MULTIPLE-CHOICE

*1. Which of the following is required in order to make a diagnosis of schizophrenia?
   a. hallucinations
   b. disorganized speech
   c. delusions
   d. none of the above

2. Formal thought disorder in schizophrenia refers to
   a. delusions.
   b. anhedonia.
   c. disorganized speech.
   d. hallucinations.

3. Which of the following are examples of negative symptoms of schizophrenia?
   a. blunted emotions, lack of initiative
   b. hallucinations and delusions
   c. difficulty concentrating, low intelligence, poor memory
   d. catatonic immobility, waxy flexibility

4. Mr. Hart spends long hours sitting in a chair with his arms behind his back and his left leg tucked under. No matter what is going on around him, he remains in this position. This is an example of which symptom of schizophrenia?
   a. somatic passivity
   b. waxy flexibility
   c. catatonic immobility
   d. inappropriate affect

5. Family studies of the genetic basis for schizophrenia look at
   a. the rate of schizophrenia in relatives of schizophrenic patients.
   b. concordance for schizophrenia in cultures where incest is relatively common.
   c. the likelihood that a schizophrenic patient will have children.
   d. the effects of being raised by a schizophrenic parent.

6. Dopamine receptors appear responsible for
   a. primarily positive symptoms.
   b. primarily negative symptoms.
   c. the onset, but not the maintenance, of schizophrenia.
   d. the maintenance, but not the onset, of schizophrenia.

7. The social selection theory proposes that
   a. poverty causes schizophrenia.
   b. schizophrenia causes poverty.
   c. social discrimination causes both schizophrenia and poverty.
   d. poverty and schizophrenia are not related.

8. Data on expressed emotion (EE) indicate that schizophrenics are more likely to relapse (that is, return to the hospital) if their families
   a. are cool, calm, unemotional and aloof.
   b. are uninvolved.
   c. are critical and overinvolved with them.
   d. provide excessive emotional support and encouragement.

9. Extrapyramidal side effects primarily affect __________ functioning.
   a. visual
   b. auditory
   c. motor
   d. cognitive

10. Which of the following is currently a general trend in the treatment of schizophrenia?
   a. community monitoring of disruptive behaviors
   b. research into improved medications
   c. guaranteed access to hospital care
   d. education and support for families

SHORT ANSWER

1. Describe five negative symptoms of schizophrenia.

2. What characteristics of the problem were emphasized by (a) Kraepelin's term "dementia praecox" and (b) Bleuler's term "schizophrenia?"

3. Why does DSM-IV's definition of schizophrenia require that the patient have symptoms for at least six months?

4. What diagnosis is appropriate for John? He believes he has the instant answer to all the country's problems. When people avoid him (because he constantly lectures them on the topic) he decides they fear the president will hear his ideas and instantly implement them. The president happened to be in town and John walked in assuming the president had come specifically to see him. When body guards threw him out, he became irate and declared the president was having sex with his wife and, thus, had refused to see him.

5. What has happened as a result of the low reliability of DSM-IV subcategories of schizophrenia?

6. Identify three weaknesses to the current dopamine theory of schizophrenia.

7. Why is it significant that schizophrenics may have enlarged ventricles?

8. Summarize data suggesting that viral complications contribute to neurological changes in schizophrenia.

9. Explain what the text means in saying that the relation between schizophrenia and social class is not a continuous progression.

10. What do "case managers" do in treating schizophrenia and why?

◆ ANSWERS TO SELF-TEST, CHAPTER 11

MULTIPLE-CHOICE

1. d (p. 283)	2. c (p. 284)	3. a (p. 286)	4. c (p. 287)
5. a (p. 293)	6. a (p. 296)	7. b (p. 300)	8. c (p. 302)
9. c (p. 305)	10. d (p. 312)		

SHORT ANSWER

1. (a) avolition or apathy, (b) alogia or slow and limited speech with little content, (c) anhedonia or not enjoying anything, (d) flat affect or lack of emotional response, (e) asociality or poor social skills and few friends. (p. 286–287)

2. (a) early onset and progressive intellectual deterioration, (b) underlying difficulty in thinking and communication. (p. 288)

3. This was part of the move to a narrower, more Kraepelinian, definition. People who abruptly develop symptoms typically recover within six months and, now, receive another diagnosis. (p. 289)

4. Paranoid schizophrenia. (p. 290–291)

5. There is much interest in finding better ways to subdivide schizophrenia, perhaps by distinguishing schizophrenics with positive, negative, and mixed symptoms. (p. 291)

6. (a) drugs block dopamine receptors quickly but take weeks to relieve symptoms, (b) to be effective, drugs must reduce dopamine to below normal, (c) newer drugs affect other neurotransmitters. (p. 297)

7. If ventricles (or brain openings) are enlarged, then the brain has shrunk. Evidence is that the loss is in subcortical areas such as the prefrontal cortex. (p. 298)

8. Schizophrenia was more common in people whose mothers were exposed to the influenza virus during their second trimester of pregnancy. (p. 300)

9. Schizophrenia is decidedly (not just relatively) more common in the lowest social classes. (p. 300)

10. They coordinate the services provided by a team and others in the community. Research shows that intensive, coordinated, community services reduce hospitalization costs and improve adjustment in many areas. (p. 312)

Chapter 12

Substance-Related Disorders

◆ OVERVIEW

The previous two chapters covered mood disorders and schizophrenia. Similar, complex physiological theories have developed around each. Physiological research and theory for the remaining disorders are not as extensive.

The next three chapters discuss disorders that have strong social and behavioral components. Chapter 12 discusses substance-related disorders including abuse of alcohol, nicotine, marijuana, and hard drugs. Chapter 13 covers personality disorders in which persistent and maladaptive personality traits or behaviors cause difficulty for the individual and others. The most well known personality disorder is the antisocial personality or psychopath characterized by antisocial behavior and/or by lack of guilt over that behavior. Chapter 14 will discuss a wide range of disorders involving sexual behavior.

Many of these problems involve behaviors that are maladaptive or socially unacceptable but not necessarily "disordered" in the traditional sense. Many are more bothersome to others than to the person involved. At times it can be difficult to decide if they are psychological, legal, or moral/ethical problems. This can present dilemmas for treatment personnel.

The text's coverage of specific problems will conclude with Chapters 15 and 16, which deal with issues and disorders of childhood and old age.

CHAPTER SUMMARY

Drugs have always been used, and abused, to alter mood and consciousness. Contemporary practice distinguishes between substance abuse that affects daily functioning and substance dependence that also produces physiological changes leading to physical tolerance (or decreasing effects) and withdrawal reactions. The chapter describes effects of five groups of commonly abused substances.

Alcohol Abuse and Dependence is a widespread social problem. Alcohol produces short-term effects including poor judgment and coordination and long-term effects including addiction and physical deterioration.

Nicotine and Cigarette Smoking is still common despite strong evidence of health risks. *Marijuana* produces a "high" characterized by decreased cognitive and psychomotor functioning. Long-term use has physical and psychological effects. Debate continues over its possible uses in medical treatment.

Sedatives and Stimulants which, respectively, decrease and increase responsiveness, include several illegal and addictive drugs. *LSD and Other Hallucinogens* were originally studied, and are now abused, for their mind-altering properties.

Research into *The Etiology of Substance Abuse and Dependence* has identified cultural, psychological, and biological variables. For example individual beliefs about the drug's effects and general personality variables influence alcohol's effects.

Therapy for Alcohol Abuse and Dependence includes detoxification followed by a number of possible therapies, each of which is only modestly effective. Similarly *Therapy for the Use of Illicit Drugs* via biological and/or psychological approaches is of limited effectiveness. *Treatment of Cigarette Smoking* describes psychological and biological treatments that are effective in smoking cessation, however, relapse is a major problem.

Prevention of Substance Abuse notes the social and pragmatic value of prevention programs, especially those directed at adolescents. Tobacco prevention programs, in particular, are common and effective methods are becoming apparent.

ESSENTIAL CONCEPTS

1. Substance abuse involves use of a drug to the extent that it interferes with functioning. Substance dependence involves more serious interference plus withdrawal reactions and increased tolerance.

2. Alcohol is an addicting drug that exacts a high cost from many individuals and from our society.

3. Alcohol's short-term physiological effects are complex and mediated by cognitive expectancies. The long-term consequences can be quite severe both psychologically and biologically.

4. Cigarette smoking is a tremendous health problem for smokers, for those near them, and for society at large.

5. Marijuana interferes with cognitive functioning and psychomotor performance and appears to have some adverse physical effects with long-term use. Its therapeutic use is controversial.

6. Sedatives or "downers" reduce the body's responsiveness. They include organic narcotics and synthetic barbiturates.

7. Sedatives are highly addicting and have important social consequences. For example, criminal behavior may result from an addict's attempt to maintain the expensive habit.

8. Stimulants (amphetamines and cocaine) are "uppers" that heighten alertness and increase autonomic activity. They are considered addictive.

9. LSD and other hallucinogens produce a state that was once thought to mimic psychosis, and is characterized sometimes by dramatic changes in perception and cognition.

10. Sociocultural, psychological, and biological factors contribute to starting and continuing abuse.

11. Therapy for alcohol and drug abuse usually begins with detoxification. Various biological and psychological therapies are difficult to evaluate but only modestly effective.

12. Most ex-smokers quit spontaneously. Psychological and biological approaches are effective in the short run; however, relapse is an issue.

13. Prevention remains the most effective approach to controlling substance abuse. Effective prevention programs are growing, especially in preventing tobacco use.

KEY TERMS

Substance dependence (p. 318)

Tolerance (p. 318)

Withdrawal (p. 318)

Substance abuse (p. 318)

Delirium tremens (DTs) (p. 319)

Polydrug abuse (p. 320)

Fetal alcohol syndrome (p. 323)

Nicotine (p. 324)

Secondhand smoke (p. 325)

Marijuana (p. 326)

Hashish (p. 326)

Sedatives (p. 330)

Opiates (p. 330

Opium (p. 330)

Morphine (p. 330)

Heroin (p. 330)

Barbiturates (p. 331)

Stimulants (p. 332)

Amphetamines (p. 332)

Cocaine (p. 333)

LSD (p. 334)

Hallucinogen (p. 335)

Mescaline (p. 335)

Psilocybin (p. 335)

Ecstasy (p. 336)

Nitrous oxide (p. 336)

Flashbacks (p. 337)

Detoxification (p. 343)

Antabuse (p. 343)

Covert sensitization (p. 345)

Controlled drinking (p. 346)

Heroin substitutes (p. 349)

Heroin antagonists (p. 349)

Methadone (p. 349)

Cross-dependent (p. 349)

Clonidine (p. 349)

◆ STUDY QUESTIONS

1. Identify and distinguish between substance dependence and substance abuse in DSM-IV. (p. 318–319)

ALCOHOL ABUSE AND DEPENDENCE (p. 319–323)

2. What are the indicators of alcohol dependence and alcohol abuse? (p. 319–320) Describe the short-term and long-term effects of alcohol abuse. (p. 321–323)

NICOTINE AND CIGARETTE SMOKING (p. 323–326)

3. How prevalent and serious is smoking? What are the consequences of smoking, especially for nonsmokers? (p. 323–326)

MARIJUANA (p. 326–329)

4. Describe changes in prevalence of marijuana use. Describe the psychological, somatic, and therapeutic effects of marijuana. (p. 326–329)

SEDATIVES AND STIMULANTS (p. 329–334)

5. The text identifies two groups of sedatives and two groups of stimulants. For each group, describe (a) short-term effects, (b) long-term effects, and (c) withdrawal effects. (p. 329–334)

LSD AND OTHER HALLUCINOGENS (p. 334–337)

6. Summarize the history of LSD and other hallucinogens. What are the general effects of hallucinogens and what variables influence their effects? (p. 334–337)

ETIOLOGY OF SUBSTANCE ABUSE AND DEPENDENCE (p. 337–342)

7. Why is the etiology of substance abuse and dependence a complex topic to study? Identify five sociocultural variables affecting alcoholism and drug abuse (starting with cross-national variations). Describe three psychological variables (including three personality factors) affecting drug use. (p. 337–341)

8. Summarize studies suggesting a biological diathesis for alcoholism. What may be the nature of this diathesis? (p. 341–342)

THERAPY FOR ALCOHOL ABUSE AND DEPENDENCE (p. 342–347)

9. Why is admitting the problem often an issue with alcoholics? Describe and evaluate traditional hospital treatment of alcoholism. Briefly describe and evaluate five treatments for alcoholism (including three variations on cognitive/behavioral methods). Identify four, more general, clinical considerations in treating alcoholics. (p. 342–347)

THERAPY FOR THE USE OF ILLICIT DRUGS (p. 347–351)

10. What is the central or first step in treating drug addiction? Describe and evaluate two biological and three psychological treatments for drug abuse. (p. 347–351)

TREATMENT OF CIGARETTE SMOKING (p. 351–354)

11. How do most people quit smoking? Illustrate the range of psychological treatments for smoking and discuss their effectiveness. Identify two biological treatments for smoking and discuss their effectiveness. What is relapse prevention? (p. 351–354)

PREVENTION OF SUBSTANCE ABUSE (p. 354–355)

12. Discuss the rationale of prevention programs generally. Describe seven common components of tobacco prevention programs (and note which one is counterproductive). (p. 354–355)

◆ SELF-TEST, CHAPTER 12

(* Items not covered in Study Questions.)

MULTIPLE-CHOICE

1. Wanda drinks frequently and now does not require as much alcohol as six months ago to achieve the same effect. She reports that she can outdrink most people. Wanda is probably
   a. genetically not predisposed to alcoholism.
   b. developing a physiological dependence on alcohol.
   c. acquiring behavioral skills in modulating her drinking.
   d. deluding herself. This is not physically possible.

*2. Most recent research on patterns of alcohol use suggests
   a. drinking is usually heaviest on weekends.
   b. that alcoholics typically alternate between binge episodes and relatively light drinking.
   c. that drinking follows well-demarcated stages.
   d. that there is no single pattern of alcohol abuse.

3. Alcohol goes into the __________ and is absorbed into the blood, after which it is metabolized by the __________ .
   a. small intestine; kidneys
   b. small intestine; liver
   c. stomach; liver
   d. stomach; kidneys

*4. Hashish is
   a. derived from resin after smoking marijuana.
   b. derived from resin from higher quality cannabis plants.
   c. based upon a mixture of marijuana and heroin.
   d. milder than marijuana.

5. The benefit of marijuana when used for chronic illnesses is primarily
   a. to reduce nausea for patients undergoing chemotherapy.
   b. to increase immune function.
   c. to improve attention and maintain medication adherence.
   d. to prevent additional infection.

6. Mark is experiencing the following symptoms after taking a drug: he feels an initial rush of ecstasy, has great self-confidence and has lost all his worries and fears. At the same time, he is feeling drowsy and relaxed. Which of the following drugs is Mark most likely to have taken recently?
   a. heroin
   b. alcohol
   c. marijuana
   d. cocaine

7. An important sociocultural variable that is cited in the increased use of cigarettes is
   a. the role of the family in providing implicit messages regarding smoking.
   b. rebound effects from the end of "just say no" campaigns.
   c. the media and advertising.
   d. the restriction of places where one may smoke.

8. Although it has been shown that alcohol does not have a consistent effect upon stress, people continue to drink as a means to alleviate stress because
   a. they expect it to help.
   b. others suggest drinking to unwind.
   c. drinking is more socially acceptable than consuming other drugs.
   d. they are unaware of the severity of life stress they are experiencing.

9. The treatment goal of Alcoholics Anonymous is
   a. to cope with their spouse's or parent's drinking.
   b. to change the public's perceptions of alcohol and alcoholism.
   c. to learn to drink socially without becoming drunk.
   d. complete abstinence from drinking.

10. "Controlled drinking" refers to
   a. using aversion therapy to control the drinking of alcoholics.
   b. the approach to alcohol use promoted by Alcoholics Anonymous.
   c. programs designed to teach alcoholics to drink in moderation rather than abstain completely.
   d. preventing alcoholism through changes in society and laws such as prohibition.

SHORT ANSWER

1. How serious a health problem is cigarette smoking?

2. What are the withdrawal effects of opium-based narcotics?

3. What events led to LSD being popularized in the 1960s?

4. Identify a number of sociocultural variables in alcoholism.

5. What is inherited as the genetic predisposition to alcoholism?

6. Disulfiram or Antabuse can discourage alcoholics from drinking by . . .

7. What is the central or first step in treating drug addiction and why?

8. What happens in self-help programs for drug addiction?

9. How effective are biological treatments for cigarette smoking?

10. What is the rationale of prevention programs?

◆ ANSWERS TO SELF-TEST, CHAPTER 12

MULTIPLE-CHOICE

1. b (p. 318)	2. d (p. 321)	3. b (p. 321)	4. b (p. 326)
5. a (p. 329)	6. a (p. 330)	7. c (p. 339)	8. a (p. 340)
9. d (p. 344)	10. c (p. 346)		

SHORT ANSWER

1. Smoking accounts for 1 in 6 deaths and is the largest preventable cause of premature death. (p. 324)

2. Withdrawal effects resemble influenza and include sneezing, sweating, and (later) cramps, chills, sleeplessness. Diarrhea and vomiting may occur. (p. 330–331)

3. Harvard LSD researchers began using it themselves, leading to a scandal. They were dismissed from Harvard and founded an organization that publicized and popularized LSD. (p. 335)

4. Cross-cultural differences, availability, family, peer pressure, media. (p. 338–339)

5. Inherit the ability to tolerate and drink large quantities of alcohol. (p. 341)

6. Produces violent vomiting if one drinks alcohol after taking it. (p. 343)

7. Detoxification or withdrawal from the drug, often under medical supervision as effects can be unpleasant and, sometimes, life threatening. (p. 347–348)

8. Residential programs remove addicts from social pressures, support nonuse, provide charismatic role models, include confrontive group therapy, respect addicts as human beings. (p. 351)

9. Research indicates they are of some, but limited, help. They work best when combined with behavioral treatments for psychological factors. (p. 353)

10. Prevention, especially with adolescents, is much easier and more effective than treatment after the problem develops. (p. 354)

Chapter 13

Personality Disorders

◆ OVERVIEW

This is the second of three chapters on problems characterized by socially problematic behaviors or traits. Generally, these are not considered "mental illnesses" as the term is commonly used. However they do cause considerable unhappiness for affected individuals and/or for those around them.

Chapter 12 covered substance-related problems including alcohol and drug abuse and dependence. Chapter 13 discusses personality disorders in which people exhibit long-term patterns of thought and behavior that are ineffective, maladaptive, or socially unacceptable. Examples include social withdrawal, self-centeredness, and criminal activity. Chapter 14 will deal with problematic sexual behaviors. These include sexual disorders or deviations, such as fetishism and rape, as well as sexual dysfunctions or inadequacies such as impotence.

Many of the problems in these chapters are characterized by socially disapproved behaviors. Often others want the person to change more than the person him or herself. This raises difficult issues. Can (or should) psychologists change people who do not especially seek change? Are psychologists acting as helpers, as law enforcers, or as moral authorities? Such issues are difficult to answer.

After Chapter 14, the next two chapters cover disorders and issues of childhood (Chapter 15) and old age (Chapter 16). They will complete the text's discussion of psychological disorders. In Chapters 17 and 18 the text will turn to general issues in abnormal psychology.

CHAPTER SUMMARY

Personality disorders are long-standing, pervasive, inflexible patterns that impair the individual's functioning in society. *Classifying Personality Disorders; Clusters, Categories, and Problems* presents basic issues in categorizing and applying these labels reliably.

In DSM, personality disorders are organized into three clusters. The *Odd/Eccentric Cluster* consists of the paranoid, schizoid, and schizotypal personality disorders. All three have characteristics that seem related to schizophrenia although research evidence is limited.

The *Dramatic/Erratic Cluster* consists of borderline, histrionic, narcissistic, and antisocial personality disorders. Various theories suggest that all result from forms of distorted and limited parent/child relationships. Antisocial personality disorder is similar to the concept of psychopathy. Research suggests that psychopaths come from families that provided little discipline, love, or effective role models. They experience limited anxiety or empathy in research studies.

The *Anxious/Fearful Cluster* consists of avoidant, dependent, and obsessive-compulsive personality disorders. Their causes are not widely studied.

Therapies for Personality Disorders have evolved out of clinical practice rather than research knowledge. Borderline personalities present major challenges and a number of therapists have adapted therapy approaches for them. Psychological and somatic treatment of psychopaths has been unsuccessful. Prisons remain the common way of handling psychopaths but are used primarily to punish and isolate them.

ESSENTIAL CONCEPTS

1. Personality disorders are characterized by inflexible and pervasive traits that interfere with functioning. These Axis II diagnoses are problematic and dimensional classification may help.

2. Ten personality disorders are defined in DSM-IV organized into three clusters.

3. Paranoid, schizoid, and schizotypal personality disorders (the odd/eccentric cluster) have unusual or withdrawn behaviors reminiscent of schizophrenia although research support is limited.

4. Borderline, histrionic, narcissistic, and antisocial personality disorders comprise the dramatic/erratic cluster. Childhood problems have been suspected in these disorders.

5. Antisocial personality disorder is related to psychopathy which has been widely studied.

6. Research indicates that psychopaths come from families with antisocial role models, poor discipline, and little love. They experience little anxiety or empathy. In fact, they appear to suppress anxiety.

7. Avoidant, dependent, and obsessive-compulsive personality disorders (the anxious/fearful cluster) are not well understood.

8. Therapies for personality disorders have developed out of the experiences of therapists working with them.

9. Borderline personalities present particular challenges for therapists. A number of therapists have developed particular therapy approaches for borderlines.

10. Efforts to change antisocial personality disorders have been unsuccessful. Psychotherapeutic and drug approaches have been of limited value. Prisons isolate psychopaths but do little to change their behavior after release.

KEY TERMS

Personality disorders (p. 358)

Paranoid personality (p. 360)

Schizoid personality (p. 360)

Schizotypal personality (p. 361)

Borderline personality (p. 361)

Histrionic personality (p. 364)

Narcissistic personality (p. 364)

Antisocial personality (p. 365)

Psychopathy (p. 366)

Avoidant personality (p. 371)

Dependent personality (p. 371)

Obsessive-compulsive personality (p. 371)

Dialectical behavior therapy (p. 376)

◆ STUDY QUESTIONS

1. Define personality disorders as a group. How are they different from normal personality styles? (p. 358)

CLASSIFYING PERSONALITY DISORDERS: CLUSTERS, CATEGORIES, AND PROBLEMS (p. 359–360)

2. Why are personality disorders placed on Axis II of DSM-IV? Identify two problems in applying these diagnoses and explain how dimensional classification may help. (p. 359–360) Identify the three clusters of personality disorders (starting on pages 360, 361, and 370).

ODD/ECCENTRIC CLUSTER (p. 360–361)

3. Identify and briefly describe the three disorders in the odd/eccentric cluster. What idea has guided the search for causes of these disorders and how well has this idea proven out so far? (p. 360–361)

DRAMATIC/ERRATIC CLUSTER (p. 361–370)

4. For borderline personality disorder, describe the disorder and three views on its etiology. For the next two disorders, describe the disorder and summarize a psychoanalytic view of its etiology. (p. 361–365)

5. Define (and distinguish between) the terms "antisocial personality disorder" and "psychopathy." Summarize data on family background and genetic factors in psychopathy. Why is it desirable to have data on the role of the family that is not retrospective? (p. 365–369)

6. Regarding emotion and psychopathy, summarize research in three areas indicating little anxiety in psychopaths and in one area indicating little empathy. Also summarize research on response modulation indicating that psychopaths respond impulsively. (p. 369–370)

ANXIOUS/FEARFUL CLUSTER (p. 370–374)

7. Briefly describe the three disorders in the anxious/fearful cluster. Give a speculated cause for each of the three disorders. (p. 370–374)

THERAPIES FOR PERSONALITY DISORDERS (p. 374–378)

8. How have therapies for personality disorders been developed generally? How have dynamic, behavioral, and cognitive therapists adapted their approaches to work with personality disorders? (p. 374)

9. Why is therapy with borderline personalities especially difficult? Describe two approaches to therapy for borderline personalities with two or three techniques of each approach. Explain what is meant by saying that the goal of therapy with personality disorders should be to change a "disorder" into a "style." (p. 375–377)

10. How effective is psychotherapy with psychopaths and why? Describe the effectiveness of imprisonment in treating psychopaths in two points. (p. 377–378)

◆ SELF-TEST, CHAPTER 13

(* Items not covered in Study Questions.)

MULTIPLE-CHOICE

1. Personality disorders differ from normal personality traits by involving
   a. long standing and dysfunctional behavior.
   b. a loss of contact with reality.
   c. personality traits that have become antisocial in nature.
   d. All of the above choices are correct.

2. A major problem that remains in diagnosing personality disorders is
   a. low reliability over time.
   b. poor interrater reliability.
   c. unstructured diagnostic criteria.
   d. very low occurrence in the population for most of the disorders.

*3. The biggest problem with the diagnosis of schizotypal personality disorder is
   a. lack of reliability in making the diagnosis.
   b. difficulty distinguishing it from schizophrenia.
   c. it is so rare that it is not clear that the disorder should be listed.
   d. overlap with other personality disorder diagnoses.

4. In object relations theory, "splitting" refers to the tendency of borderline personality disorders to
   a. separate themselves from society.
   b. forget unpleasant events.
   c. see people as all good or all bad.
   d. think illogically.

5. Cleckley emphasized which of the following aspects of antisocial personality that is *not* emphasized in DSM-IV?
   a. acting out as a child
   b. lack of shame or guilt
   c. reckless and aggressive
   d. impulsive antisocial acts

6. In research on response modulation and psychopathy, psychopaths won or lost money depending on what playing cards appeared. In this research, the impulsivity of psychopaths was studied by
   a. making them wait before deciding to continue the game.
   b. having them estimate the amount of money they had won.
   c. ratings of their verbal statements during the game.
   d. All of the above are correct.

*7. High rates of which DSM diagnosis have been found in the individuals with dependent personality disorder?
   a. depression
   b. schizophrenia
   c. somatization disorder
   d. dissociative identity disorder

8. Behavior and cognitive therapists have generally treated most forms of personality disorder by
   a. redefining the problem in more behavioral terms.
   b. doing cognitive therapy that emphasizes that behavior is state-like and not trait-like.
   c. using money as a reinforcer to shape socially desirable behavior.
   d. working with teachers as a prevention measure for future instances of personality disorders.

9. Dialectical behavior therapy for patients with borderline personality disorder combines
   a. social skills training and free-association.
   b. ego analysis and more directive behavioral techniques.
   c. behavioral problem-solving and client-centered empathy.
   d. Gestalt techniques and relaxation training.

10. Psychotherapy with psychopaths is difficult because
   a. their speech patterns are difficult to understand.
   b. they are unable to explain reasons for their behavior.
   c. therapists are required to report any past misdeeds.
   d. they do not form open relationships with therapists.

SHORT ANSWER

1. Define "personality disorders" (as a group).

2. Why are personality disorders placed on a different axis of DSM IV?

3. Distinguish between schizoid personality and schizotypal personality.

4. How are histrionic and narcissistic personality disorder the same and different?

5. Research on the role of the family finds that psychopaths tend to come from families characterized by . . .

6. Describe research on response modulation showing impulsivity in psychopaths.

7. What is the (speculated) basis of obsessive-compulsive personality disorder?

8. In general, how have therapies for personality disorders been developed?

9. What does it mean to say that the goal of therapy should be to change disorders into styles?

10. How effective is the standard treatment for psychopaths?

◆ ANSWERS TO SELF-TEST, CHAPTER 13

MULTIPLE-CHOICE

1. a (p. 358)	2. a (p. 359)	3. d (p. 361)	4. c (p. 363)
5. b (p. 366)	6. a (p. 370)	7. a (p. 371)	8. a (p. 374)
9. c (p. 376)	10. d (p. 377)		

SHORT ANSWER

1. Characterized by enduring, inflexible patterns of inner experience and behavior that deviate from cultural expectations and cause distress or impairment. (p. 358)

2. To remind clinicians to consider their possible presence (in addition to Axis I disorders, which are often the reason the person seeks help). (p. 359)

3. Both have few close friends but in addition schizotypal personality has eccentric ideas, mannerisms, appearance, etc. (p. 361)

4. Both are self-centered. Seemingly histrionics seek to prove they are special (seek to impress others, etc.) while narcissistics are convinced they already are special (deserve special attention, etc.). (p. 364–365)

5. Rejection, lack of affection, inconsistent discipline, antisocial fathers. (p. 368)

6. In a card game where the odds of winning decreased steadily, psychopaths continued to play (and lose) longer than normals — unless required to wait 5 seconds before deciding whether to continue. (p. 370)

7. They are overcompensating for fear of loss of control by pushing to control as much of their life as possible. (p. 373–374)

8. Developed by practicing clinicians who report on people they have treated. Not based on formal research. (p. 374)

9. The goal should be not to change the person's basic approach to life but to help the person express it in more adaptive, moderate, flexible ways. (p. 377)

10. The standard treatment (prison) is not very effective at all. In fact, criminologists have argued that prisons are schools for crime. (p. 378)

Chapter 14

Sexual and Gender Identity Disorders

◆ OVERVIEW

Chapter 14 is the last of three chapters on problems with a social emphasis. Generally these are not considered "mental illnesses" as such but involve particular behaviors or traits that are of concern to society as well as, sometimes, to the individual. Chapter 12 discussed substance abuse problems that concern both society and the individual to varying degrees. Social and individual concerns about these problems can change dramatically as has happened with cigarette smoking. Chapter 13 discussed personality disorders. Many of these, especially antisocial personality disorders, are clearly more a "problem" for society than for the individual criminal.

Chapter 14 covers sexual problems. Sexual deviations, as the term implies, refer to sexual activities that society considers deviant or aberrant. Like the personality disorders and substance abuse disorders of the last two chapters, defining a sexual activity as "deviant" involves a value judgment. Again our social and individual concerns may change as has happened regarding homosexuality. Sexual dysfunctions are much more common sexual problems involving inhibitions of sexual functioning. Sexual dysfunctions include premature orgasm, vaginismus, and inhibited sexual desire or arousal.

Chapter 14 is the last chapter focusing on socially problematic behaviors. The next two chapters discuss issues and problems of childhood (Chapter 15) and of old age (Chapter 16). Then the text concludes with two chapters on treatment and legal/ethical issues.

CHAPTER SUMMARY

In *Gender Identity Disorder* individuals have a sense of themselves as being of one sex although they are, anatomically, the other sex. Such individuals may seek sex-change surgery to make their physical anatomy consistent with their inner sense of themselves. Behavior therapy can also help them change their behaviors, sexual fantasies, etc., to match their anatomy.

The Paraphilias involve unusual sexual activities or fantasies that the individual either acts on or is markedly disturbed by. They may involve sexual gratification through intimate articles, cross dressing, or through sexual activities involving pain, children, strangers, etc. Theories of paraphilias often suggest multiple ways they could develop. Behavior therapists treat such problems using aversion therapy to reduce the unwanted attraction plus social skills training to enable normal sexual relations.

Rape is more an act of violence than of sex. Many professionals view it as a result of social stereotypes. Treatment of rapists is difficult and attention focuses on helping victims cope with the trauma.

The Sexual Dysfunctions describes dysfunctions as persistent and recurrent inhibitions in sexual functioning that may develop at each stage of the human sexual response cycle. While organic factors may be involved, psychological factors are usually central. Masters and Johnson theorize that historical factors, such as early sexual teachings and experiences, may lead the individual to develop performance fears or adopt a spectator role thus inhibiting full participation in sexual activities. Therapies for sexual dysfunctions are highly effective. They focus both on sexual skills and on the relationship.

ESSENTIAL CONCEPTS

1. Gender identity disorders involve feeling that one is the opposite of one's anatomical sex.
2. The two major treatments for gender identity disorders (sex-change surgery and alterations in gender identity) remain controversial.
3. Paraphilias involve a deviation in the object of sexual arousal.
4. The more common paraphilias include fetishism, transvestic fetishism, incest, pedophilia, voyeurism, exhibitionism, sadism, and masochism.
5. Treatment of paraphilias has focused on the behavior itself via behavioral therapy and judicial interventions. Their effectiveness is unclear and suggests a multifaceted approach is needed.
6. Rape is often more a crime of aggression and dominance and can have a tremendously adverse impact on the victim.
7. Sexual dysfunctions are inhibitions or disturbances in one of four phases of the human sexual response cycle.
8. The sexual response cycle is described as having appetitive, excitement, orgasm, and resolution phases.
9. Sexual dysfunctions include (in the appetitive phase) hypoactive sexual desire and sexual aversion; (in the excitement phase) female arousal and male erectile disorders; (in the orgasm phase) female or male orgasmic disorders, and premature ejaculation; as well as sexual pain disorders of vaginismus, and dyspareunia.
10. Masters and Johnson proposed that historical factors lead to current factors (performance fears and the spectator role) resulting in sexual dysfunctions.
11. Behavioral and cognitive treatments for sexual dysfunctions are very effective. They include anxiety reduction, education, frank discussion about sexuality, and specific techniques for treating dysfunctions.

KEY TERMS

Sexual and gender identity disorders (p. 381)

Gender identity (p. 381)

Transsexualism [Gender identity disorder — GID] (p. 382)

Sex-reassignment surgery (p. 384)

Paraphilias (p. 387)

Fetishism (p. 387)

Transvestic fetishism (p. 387)

Pedophilia (p. 388)

Incest (p. 388)

Voyeurism [peeping] (p. 390)

Exhibitionism (p. 391)

Frotteurism (p. 391)

Sexual sadism (p. 391)

Sexual masochism (p. 391)

Child sexual abuse [CSA] (p. 392)

Orgasmic reorientation (p. 397)

Forced rape (p. 398)

Statutory rape (p. 398)

Acquaintance [date] rape (p. 399)

Sexual dysfunctions (p. 402)

Homosexuality (p. 404)

Ego-dystonic homosexuality (p. 404)

Homophobia (p. 404)

Hypoactive sexual desire disorder (p. 405)

Sexual aversion disorder (p. 405)

Female sexual arousal disorder (p. 406)

Male erectile disorder (p. 406)

Female orgasmic disorder (p. 407)

Male orgasmic disorder (p. 408)

Premature ejaculation (p. 408)

Dyspareunia (p. 409)

Vaginismus (p. 409)

Fears of performance (p. 410)

Spectator role (p. 410)

Secondary gain (p. 411)

Sensory-awareness procedures (p. 412)

Sexual value system (p. 414)

Sensate focus (p. 414)

◆ STUDY QUESTIONS

1. Identify and distinguish among the three kinds of sexual problems discussed in this chapter. (p. 381)

GENDER IDENTITY DISORDERS (p. 381–387)

2. Define gender identity disorder (GID) noting it is based on inner beliefs. Summarize evidence that hormonal problems and family factors are (and are not) involved. How do cultural values complicate this topic? (p. 381–384)

3. Describe the steps in treating GID by altering the body. Does this treatment appear effective (and why is its effectiveness difficult to evaluate)? Describe an alternative treatment altering psychology and its effectiveness. (p. 384–387)

THE PARAPHILIAS (p. 387–402)

4. Define paraphilias as a group of disorders. Discuss issues around the terms "recurrent" and "distressed" as opposed to arrest-based definitions. Define seven types of paraphilias and the background or personality factors usually associated with each. (p. 387–395)

5. Summarize perspectives on the etiology of the paraphilias including one psychodynamic, four behavioral/cognitive, and one biological perspective. (p. 395–396)

6. Describe two general issues in treatment of paraphilias. What has been the impact of psychoanalytic approaches? Describe a range of behavioral and cognitive treatments and their overall effectiveness. Describe biological treatments and issues in their use. Describe Megan's Law as a preventive measure and its unintended consequence. (p. 396–398)

RAPE (p. 398–402)

7. Is rape a sexual crime? Explain. What are the effects of rape on victims during and after the attack? Identify common motivations of rapists. (p. 398–401)

8. Describe the common approach to treating rapists and its effectiveness. What are the immediate and long-term goals in counseling rape victims? (p. 401–402)

SEXUAL DYSFUNCTIONS (p. 402–415)

9. How are sexual dysfunctions different from other sexual problems discussed earlier? Identify four phases of the human sexual response cycle. (p. 402–405)

10. How common are occasional disturbances in sexual functioning and when are they labeled dysfunctions? Describe nine sexual dysfunctions organized into four categories. (Note the parallels between these categories and the phases of the human sexual response cycle.) Identify common causes of each dysfunction. (p. 405–409)

11. According to Masters and Johnson, how do current and historical factors interact to result in sexual dysfunctions? Briefly describe their two current and seven historical factors. (p. 409–411)

12. Identify five factors suggested by other contemporary views and two general cautions regarding this area. (p. 411–412)

13. Briefly describe seven techniques used in treating sexual dysfunctions. Notice that, in practice, combinations of these techniques are used. (p. 412–415)

◆ SELF-TEST, CHAPTER 14

(* Items not covered in Study Questions.)

MULTIPLE-CHOICE

1. The sense of being either male or female is referred to as
   a. sexual orientation.
   b. sex role stereotype.
   c. gender identity.
   d. Oedipal identification.

2. Transsexuals are people who
   a. are attracted to members of the same sex.
   b. dress in the clothing of the opposite sex for sexual gratification.
   c. prefer the company of people of the opposite sex.
   d. identify themselves as members of the opposite sex.

3. A component of psychotherapy prior to sex-reassignment surgery involves
   a. discouraging the patient from seeking surgery, to ensure that they are serious.
   b. focusing on options available that the person may have overlooked, such as removing facial hair or reducing chin size in male to female surgery.
   c. training in proper opposite-sex behavior following surgery.
   d. examining underlying causes of opposite gender identity.

4. A behavioral hypothesis regarding the etiology of exhibitionism is based on ___________ theory.
   a. classical conditioning
   b. operant conditioning
   c. systematic desensitization
   d. modeling

*5. Rape in wartime
   a. is so common as to be expected.
   b. is a war crime.
   c. is part of a masculine superiority culture as part of war.
   d. All of the above choices are correct.

*6. Homophobia appears to be associated with
   a. child sexual abuse.
   b. unrecognized same-sex arousal.
   c. denial of one's heterosexuality.
   d. fixation at the anal stage.

7. Elizabeth is beginning to feel aroused from direct physical contact with her husband. The change in blood flow to her genital area is referred to as
   a. resolution.
   b. tumescence.
   c. appetitive response.
   d. engorgement.

8. Which of the following DSM-IV diagnosis has historically been associated with a derogatory label of "frigidity"?
   a. low sex drive
   b. dyspareunia
   c. sexual aversion disorder
   d. female orgasmic disorder

9. Joan experiences pain during sexual intercourse. The frequency of pain has been so frequent that she now dreads the prospect of possible sexual encounters despite experiencing sexual arousal while observing films depicting sexual acts. Joan most likely is suffering from
   a. female orgasmic disorder.
   b. dyspareunia.
   c. imperforate hymen.
   d. major depression.

10. Directed masturbation is often used
   a. to train individuals who have difficulty achieving orgasm.
   b. as a means for redirecting attention from inappropriate sexual stimuli.
   c. for excessive sexual appetite.
   d. as part of a program of treatment for sex offenders.

SHORT ANSWER

1. How effective is treating gender identity disorder by psychologically changing gender orientation?

2. Define paraphilias in general.

3. Define frotteurism.

4. What do most sadists and masochists think and do about their unusual sexual preferences?

5. How important are biological factors in the paraphilias?

6. Describe the behavioral approach to treatment of paraphilias.

7. What are the psychological effects of rape on the victim?

8. Describe the effectiveness of therapy for rapists.

9. Summarize other other contemporary views of the role of interpersonal factors in sexual dysfunctions.

10. List a number of components of therapy for sexual dysfunctions that do *not* focus directly on sexual activity as such.

◆ ANSWERS TO SELF-TEST, CHAPTER 14

MULTIPLE-CHOICE

1. c (p. 381)
2. d (p. 382)
3. b (p. 384–385)
4. a (p. 395)
5. d (p. 400)
6. b (p. 404–405)
7. b (p. 405)
8. d (p. 407)
9. b (p. 409)
10. a (p. 412)

SHORT ANSWER

1. Difficult to evaluate as most people refuse this approach. Several case studies indicate mixed effectiveness. (p. 396)

2. Attraction to deviant (unusual or unacceptable) sexual activities. The urges must be intense and recurrent so that the individual has acted on them or is markedly distressed by them. (p. 387)

3. Sexual touching of an unsuspecting person. (p. 391)

4. They are relatively comfortable with their preferences and find compatible partners with whom to act out their desires. (p. 394)

5. Not very important. There has been speculation but research is inconclusive. Biological factors are, at most, only one of many factors. (p. 396)

6. Procedures are tailored to the individual but often include: aversive procedures to decrease inappropriate attractions, positive conditioning of appropriate attractions, and teaching of social skills so the individual can find partners. (p. 396–397)

7. Terrified, vulnerable, and violated during attack. Afterwards tense, humiliated, angry, or guilty. Nightmares, continued fears, sexual difficulties are common. (p. 399)

8. Difficult to evaluate but probably somewhat lower recidivism. As with paraphilias, treatment often attempted in prison with minimally motivated people. (p. 401)

9. Interpersonal and sexual factors are intertwined. By the time a couple seeks help, one cannot tell whether sex or couple problems started first. (p. 411)

10. Anxiety reduction, skills & communication training, couples therapy focusing on communication issues, etc. (p. 412–413)

Chapter 15

Disorders of Childhood

◆ OVERVIEW

Chapter 14 concluded three chapters on socially problematic behaviors and traits. This is the first of two chapters devoted to developmental problems and issues. Chapter 15 covers issues and problems that arise in childhood, Chapter 16 covers issues and problems of old age. Both chapters focus on the general concerns and circumstances of young/old people in our society as well as on their psychological problems.

Disorders of childhood (this chapter) are complicated by several factors. Children are developing and changing rapidly. They have difficulty expressing their concerns or asking for help. Not surprisingly, they often receive help for problems that bother the adults around them. Typically these include misbehavior (hyperactivity and conduct disorders) and educational difficulties (learning disabilities and mental retardation). The chapter also covers childhood autism, a serious and pervasive developmental problem.

The next chapter, Chapter 16, will deal with problems of aging. Older individuals are subject to a wide variety of problems. They must cope with deterioration as well as whatever problems they may have developed over time. More importantly they must cope with the realization that they are getting older as well as the fact that society often does not seem to respect, value, or provide for them.

Chapters 15 and 16 complete the text's discussion of specific problems. The last chapters of the text focus on issues related to abnormal psychology. Chapter 17 discusses issues in psychological intervention. Chapter 18 covers legal and ethical issues. Many of these issues have been mentioned throughout the text. The last two chapters provide a more organized and extensive discussion of them.

CHAPTER SUMMARY

Classification of Childhood Disorders is complicated because, as children develop, our expectations for their behavior change.

Disorders of Undercontrolled Behavior include attention-deficit/hyperactivity disorder and conduct disorder. Children with attention-deficit/hyperactivity disorder have trouble focusing their attention, leading to difficulty in school and play activities. Conduct disorder involves acting-out behaviors such as juvenile delinquency. Both have been attributed to a wide variety of factors including biological or genetic deficits and family upbringing.

Learning Disabilities are developmental delays in specific areas (reading, etc.) not related to general intellectual retardation. Research, especially on dyslexia, has suggested problems in specific brain areas. Treatment consists of teaching specific skills.

A diagnosis of *Mental Retardation* traditionally involves three criteria: subnormal intellectual functioning, deficits in adaptive behavior, and onset before age 18. Severe retardation usually results from physical factors such as chromosomal abnormalities or brain injuries. Mild retardation with no clear cause is much more common and probably results from a combination of biological, motivational, and environmental factors. Social enrichment programs seek to prevent or minimize retardation. Educational and behavioral programs are used to treat problems of retarded individuals as well as improve their intellectual functioning.

Autistic Disorder is, fortunately, an uncommon disorder in which very young children show profound problems in speech, learning, and social relations. Research has not supported early theories which suggested that autistic children had been rejected by emotionally cold parents. Physiological causes have been suggested. Treatment of autism is difficult. Behavioral procedures using modeling and operant conditioning are promising. However, most autistic children remain intellectually and socially limited.

ESSENTIAL CONCEPTS

1. Disorders of undercontrolled behavior include hyperactivity and conduct disorders.

2. Attention-deficit/hyperactivity disorder probably has multiple causes and is characterized by inattention, impulsivity, overactivity, academic difficulties, and troubled peer relationships.

3. Conduct disorders tend to be long-lasting difficulties that resist treatment although newer behavioral and cognitive methods are promising.

4. Learning disabilities are specific developmental problems in an isolated area of academic or daily functioning.

5. Traditional diagnostic criteria for mental retardation are: (a) significantly subaverage intellectual functioning, (b) deficits in adaptive behavior, and (c) onset prior to age 18.

6. There are four classification levels of mental retardation (mild, moderate, severe, and profound), with different IQ scores and prognoses for each level.

7. The specific etiology for most cases of mental retardation is unknown. A combination of biological, motivational, and environmental factors is probably involved. These cases generally fall in the mild category.

8. More severe cases of mental retardation typically result from known physical causes including Down's syndrome, PKU, and various chemical and environmental hazards.

9. Early interventions such as Project Head Start can minimize or prevent mild mental retardation. Institutional programs and specific behavioral/cognitive programs are also used.

10. Infantile autism is characterized by extreme autistic aloneness, severely limited language, and ritualistic behavior.

11. The specific etiology of infantile autism remains unknown, although recent work suggests biological, not psychological, factors.

12. Highly structured social-learning treatments have been successful in reducing self-injury and in improving communication and self-care skills of autistic children; however, their long-term prognosis is limited.

KEY TERMS

Attention-deficit/hyperactivity disorder [ADHD] (p. 420)

Conduct disorders (p. 425)

Oppositional defiant disorder (p. 425)

Learning disabilities (p. 430)

Learning disorders (p. 430)

Reading disorder [dyslexia] (p. 430)

Disorder of written expression (p. 430)

Mathematics disorder (p. 430)

Expressive language disorder (p. 431)

Phonological disorder (p. 431)

Stuttering (p. 431)

Motor skills disorder (p. 431)

Enuresis (p. 432)

Mild mental retardation (p. 437)

Moderate mental retardation (p. 437)

Severe mental retardation (p. 437)

Profound mental retardation (p. 437)

Down's syndrome [trisomy 21] (p. 439)

Fragile X syndrome (p. 439)

Phenylketonuria (p. 440)

Applied behavior analysis (p. 442)

Self-instructional training (p. 442)

Autistic disorder (p. 443)

Pervasive developmental disorders (p. 444)

Echolalia (p. 447)

Pronoun reversal (p. 447)

◆ STUDY QUESTIONS

CLASSIFICATION OF CHILDHOOD DISORDERS (p. 418–420)

1. To classify abnormal behavior in children, what must diagnosticians consider first and why? (p. 418–420)

DISORDERS OF UNDERCONTROLLED BEHAVIOR (p. 420–430)

2. What are the characteristics of attention-deficit/hyperactivity disorder (ADHD)? Distinguish between ADHD and "rambunctious kid." Distinguish between ADHD and conduct disorder. (p. 420–422)

3. Why is no one theory or factor likely to explain all hyperactivity? Briefly list biological, environmental, and psychological factors that may contribute to hyperactivity. Describe and evaluate two treatments for hyperactivity. (p. 422–425)

4. Define conduct disorder and its possible relation to oppositional defiant disorder (ODD). Discuss the prognosis for conduct-disordered children including Moffitt's (1993) proposal. (p. 425–427)

5. Identify biological, psychological, and sociological evidence on the etiology of conduct disorder. Describe and evaluate treatment approaches based on: incarceration, family intervention, multisystem treatment, anger-control, and moral reasoning. (p. 427–430)

LEARNING DISABILITIES (p. 430–435)

6. Define seven learning disabilities in three groups. Briefly identify three physiological and three psychological possible factors in dyslexia. Identify three possible etiologies for mathematics disorder. Describe two common approaches to intervention and a common need in any intervention program. (p. 430–435)

MENTAL RETARDATION (p. 436–443)

7. Define "mental retardation" using three traditional criteria. Identify four levels of retardation in DSM-IV including the IQ range and level of social functioning for each. What other approach is encouraged by the American Association of Mental Retardation? (p. 436–438)

8. What percentage of retarded individuals have no clearly defined etiology? Identify typical intellectual and social characteristics of these individuals. For those with known etiologies, briefly describe five biological causes with an example of each. (p. 438–441)

9. Describe and evaluate five approaches to preventing and/or treating mental retardation. (p. 441–443)

AUTISTIC DISORDER (p. 443–454)

10. What is the distinguishing characteristic of autistic disorder? How do autistic and retarded individuals compare on IQ tests? Describe several characteristics of autism in each of three areas. What is the prognosis for autistic children? (p. 443–449)

11. Summarize two early psychological approaches to autism. How well has research supported them? Describe results in two research areas suggesting a biological basis for infantile autism. (p. 449–452)

12. List four special problems in treating autistic children. Describe and evaluate three general approaches to treating autism. (p. 452–454)

◆ SELF-TEST, CHAPTER 15

(* Items not covered in Study Questions.)

MULTIPLE-CHOICE

*1. The worst prognosis is for those children who have
 a. only ADHD.
 b. only conduct disorder.
 c. both ADHD and conduct disorder.
 d. All of the above have an equally poor prognosis.

2. The genetic factors that are inherited by children with ADHD are
 a. brain function and structure.
 b. neurotransmitter function and specificity.
 c. appetitive and metabolic functions.
 d. All of the above are correct.

3. Which of the following is *not* a symptom of oppositional-defiant disorder?
 a. stealing
 b. temper tantrums
 c. refusing to follow directions
 d. annoying others deliberately

4. According to Dodge and Frame (1982), aggressive children demonstrate cognitive biases in situations
 a. in which peers act aggressively.
 b. in which peers act in a prosocial manner.
 c. which are ambiguous.
 d. in which they are rejected.

*5. The bell and pad controls bed-wetting by
 a. waking the child when he or she begins wetting.
 b. waking the parents to clean the child's bed.
 c. administering a mild shock when the child begins wetting.
 d. signaling the child when his or her bladder is full.

6. The DSM-IV diagnosis of mental retardation requires both low intellectual functioning and
 a. poor social skills.
 b. poor adaptive skills.
 c. poor academic achievement.
 d. inability to hold a job.

7. Mildly retarded adults
 a. are about twice as likely to be institutionalized as nonretarded individuals.
 b. usually have learning disabilities which prevent them from attending school beyond the 6th grade.
 c. have usually learned academic skills up to about the 10th grade level, but rarely have graduated from high school.
 d. can usually work at unskilled jobs and help support themselves financially.

*8. The “bump” in the normal curve
  a. represents the number of expected cases of mentally retarded individuals in the population.
  b. is a misnomer, because there is actually an extreme flattening in the curve.
  c. is the area where there is a higher than expected number of cases of mentally retarded individuals.
  d. has not been observed in epidemiology estimates.

*9. Autism was formerly considered a form of
  a. learning disability.
  b. mental retardation.
  c. schizophrenia.
  d. conduct disorder.

10. Early behavioral theorists emphasized the role of ___________ in the etiology of autism.
  a. exposure to war or other traumas
  b. biological factors
  c. bad parenting
  d. well-meaning but overindulgent parents

SHORT ANSWER

1. What issue must be considered before diagnosing any childhood disorder?

2. Distinguish between ADHD and "rambunctious kid."

3. How effective are drug treatments for hyperactivity?

4. Describe what is done in family intervention with conduct-disordered children.

5. Summarize the evidence regarding visual perceptual deficits as a basis for dyslexia.

6. Describe PKU as a cause of mental retardation.

7. Describe the effectiveness of Head Start as a means of preventing mental retardation.

8. Describe common communication deficits of autistic children.

9. What research suggests a genetic basis for autism?

10. Summarize research on drug treatments for autism.

◆ ANSWERS TO SELF-TEST, CHAPTER 15

MULTIPLE-CHOICE

1. c (p. 422)	2. a (p. 423)	3. a (p. 425–426)	4. c (p. 428)
5. a (p. 432)	6. b (p. 436)	7. d (p. 437)	8. c (p. 438)
9. c (p. 444)	10. c (p. 449)		

SHORT ANSWER

1. What behavior is normal for the age. The "symptoms" may be typical. (p. 418)

2. Many kids are active and rambunctious. ADHD is for extreme and persistent problems, not just kids who are more active than parents or teachers prefer. (p. 421)

3. Drugs improve concentration and reduce behavior problems but have little effect on long-term academic achievement and have side-effects. (p. 424–425)

4. Parental behavior management training emphasizing positive reinforcement of prosocial behavior plus time-outs, age-appropriate consequences, etc. (p. 429)

5. Research has not supported past theories linking dyslexia to perceptual deficits such as seeing letters backwards. (p. 433)

6. PKU is a genetic inability to process phenylalanine, a protein amino acid. Without special diet phenylalanine accumulates in the body, producing brain damage and retardation. (p. 440)

7. Research shows that Head Start children improve on a variety of social and academic measures but remain behind their peers. (p. 441–442)

8. Half never speak at all. Others have speech peculiarities including echolalia, pronoun reversal, and neologisms. (p. 447–448)

9. Risk of autism rises dramatically in siblings of autistics; up to 91% in identical twins of autistics. (Cannot do family studies as autistics rarely marry.) (p. 451)

10. Several drugs have been tried with mixed success. They produce some improvement in some autistic children but have side-effects. (p. 454)

Chapter 16

Aging and Psychological Disorders

◆ OVERVIEW

Chapter 16 is the concluding chapter on developmental problems. Chapter 15 discussed disorders of childhood and growing up. Chapter 16 is devoted to the problems of aging and growing old. Both young and old people in our society are vulnerable. Others do not always think about their special circumstances and needs or provide care and attention they may need. This is more true for older than for younger people — a disturbing thought for those who plan to live long enough to grow old.

Chapter 16 completes the text's discussion of specific psychological disorders. The last two chapters of the text deal more intensively with issues in abnormal psychology. Chapter 17 evaluates various treatment methods and discusses issues in integrating them. Finally, Chapter 18 will cover legal and ethical issues. Legal issues include issues regarding the insanity defense and commitment of disturbed individuals. Ethical issues cover rights of therapy clients and research participants. Earlier chapters have mentioned these topics in various contexts. The last two chapters bring together and complete these discussions.

CHAPTER SUMMARY

Growing old is, obviously, a time of physical decline. Medical problems become an increasing concern. Beyond the purely medical aspects of old age, however, are a wide range of psychological and social problems.

The chapter begins by summarizing *Issues, Concepts, and Methods in the Study of Older Adults.* This discussion forms a basis for considering physical and psychological disorders of older adults.

Old Age and Brain Disorders covers two disorders. Dementias are slowly developing, progressive conditions that are usually irreversible and require supportive care. Deliriums develop suddenly and, if recognized, can often be reversed by treating the underlying physical conditions.

Old Age and Psychological Disorders emphasizes factors that make the elderly more (or less) susceptible to various problems. Depression often accompanies physical and psychological declines as people grow old. Anxiety problems may continue from younger years or develop as new issues emerge. Suspiciousness and paranoia may result as the elderly have difficulty understanding others due to hearing problems and social isolation. The elderly are also subject to other psychological problems. Suicide may result as they struggle to accept changing physical and social situations. Contrary to popular conceptions, older adults are capable of enjoying and engaging in sexual activity despite slowed biological responses.

Treatment and Care of Older Adults is complicated by stereotypes and misinformation among professionals. Nursing homes and other facilities often fail to encourage the elderly to maintain their skills and capabilities. Community-based services could help the elderly remain as independent as possible. *Issues Specific to Therapy with Older Adults* include changing social and personal realities. Therapists can adjust the content and process of therapy to reflect these issues.

ESSENTIAL CONCEPTS

1. Age effects, cohort effects, and time-of-measurement effects complicate research efforts to understand older adults.

2. Dementia is a gradual deterioration of intellectual abilities over several years until functioning becomes impaired.

3. Many cases of dementia are irreversible. Treatment consists of support and assistance in living as independently as possible.

4. Most dementia patients are in the care of their families and support for these families is valuable, especially when they must decide about institutionalization.

5. Delirium is a clouded state of consciousness characterized by difficulty in concentrating and maintaining a directed stream of thought. Many cases of delirium are reversible if detected in time.

6. There is a tendency to attribute the behavior of older adults to the fact that they are older. This can lead to erroneous conclusions about the effects of aging and cause us to overlook the individual's uniqueness.

7. Difficulties of growing old can contribute to psychological problems including depression, paranoid disorder, abuse of prescription drugs, and insomnia.

8. Most older adults maintain sexual interest and engage in sexual activity although there may be a general slowing of the sexual response cycle and the intensity of sexual arousal may not be as great.

9. Regardless of whether they are cared for in the community or in a nursing home, giving the aged responsibility for self-care, planning, and control over their lives is important to their continued psychological and physical well-being.

10. Psychotherapy with the elderly requires sensitivity to their special issues. The elderly can benefit from help in coping with the realistic problems of old age.

KEY TERMS

Ageism (p. 457)

Age effects (p. 460)

Cohort effects (p. 460)

Time of measurement effects (p. 460)

Cross-sectional studies (p. 460)

Longitudinal studies (p. 460)

Selective mortality (p. 461)

Dementia (p. 461)

Alzheimer's disease (p. 462)

Plaques (p. 264)

Neurofibrillary tangles (p. 462)

Delirium (p. 467)

Paraphrenia (p. 475)

Sleep apnea (p. 479)

◆ STUDY QUESTIONS

ISSUES, CONCEPTS, AND METHODS IN THE STUDY OF OLDER ADULTS (p. 459–461)

1. How does diversity change in groups of older people? Identify three effects that complicate research on aging. Include a description of factors that complicate both cross-sectional and longitudinal studies. Describe two other factors that make it difficult to know about psychological problems in older adults. (p. 459–461)

OLD AGE AND BRAIN DISORDERS (p. 461–469)

2. Define two forms of brain disorder that may affect the elderly (on p. 461 and 467). Describe common symptoms and the common cause of dementia in older adults. What are the physiological changes and genetic factors in Alzheimer's? What are the goals of treatment from biological and psychosocial perspectives? (p. 461–467)

3. Describe common symptoms of delirium and distinguish them from symptoms of dementia. What are common causes and treatment? (p. 467–469)

OLD AGE AND PSYCHOLOGICAL DISORDERS (p. 470–484)

4. Why do we tend to ignore psychological problems among the elderly — and how common are they? (p. 470) List the nine psychological problems covered in this section. (p. 470–484)

5. The text describes depression, anxiety, and delusional (paranoid) disorders. For each problem describe (a) how it differs in older people, (b) possible causes, and (c) treatment. (p. 470–474)

6. Briefly describe two or three issues for each of the following topics (a) schizophrenia, (b) alcohol abuse, (c) abuse of illegal drugs, and (d) medication misuse in older adults. (p. 474–478)

7. Describe the causes and treatment of three other psychological problems among the elderly. (p. 478–481)

8. How does sexuality change with age? Describe physiological changes for men and for women as well as general problems related to age. What is the general approach to treating sexual dysfunctions in the elderly? (p. 481–484)

TREATMENT AND CARE OF THE ELDERLY (p. 484–488)

9. Identify three general issues in treatment and care of the elderly. (p. 484)

10. What is a common effect on family caregivers of nursing home placement? Summarize a study suggesting subtle problems in nursing home care and possible reasons for the results. Identify two other reasons for poor physical and mental health care. Describe community-based care and three problems in caring for the elderly in the community. (p. 484–488)

ISSUES SPECIFIC TO THERAPY WITH OLDER ADULTS (p. 488–492)

11. Identify six content and five process issues in providing therapy to older adults. (p. 488–495)

◆ SELF-TEST, CHAPTER 16

(* Items not covered in Study Questions.)

MULTIPLE-CHOICE

*1. Setting the age at which one is considered "old," which is now 65, is based upon
  a. clear biological changes that begin at about that age.
  b. social policy.
  c. the age at which individuals begin to refer to themselves as old.
  d. a scientific standard.

2. Disorders of old-age in DSM-IV
  a. have been revised substantially from the previous DSMs.
  b. are basically the same as those of younger adults.
  c. are included in a separate section for the first time.
  d. are basically similar to Axis II disorders.

3. Plaques, which develop as part of Alzheimer's disease, are
  a. fatty deposits in areas of the brain.
  b. cholesterol remains from poor diet.
  c. remnants of lost neurons and a waxy protein.
  d. equivalent to neurofibrillary tangles.

4. Delirium can occur only
  a. after age 70.
  b. following a stroke.
  c. after a significant life stressor such as loss of a spouse.
  d. None of these are correct. Delirium can occur at any time.

5. Depression in older adults can be distinguished from depression in younger adults by higher levels of
  a. somatic complaints.
  b. suicidal ideation.
  c. hostility.
  d. agitation.

6. Paraphrenia differs from schizophrenia in that paraphrenia is associated with
  a. more negative symptoms.
  b. more hallucinations and paranoia.
  c. reduced Parkinson's from antipsychotic medications.
  d. fewer social skills deficits.

7. Epidemiologists forecast that in the years to come
  a. cannabis and heroin use will decline among older adults.
  b. fewer older adults will enter methadone treatment clinics.
  c. there will be a sharp rise in cocaine use among older adults.
  d. cannabis use will increase.

8. A side effect of sleeping pills, especially among older adults, is
   a. reduced REM sleep.
   b. insomnia.
   c. respiratory difficulties.
   d. All of the above are side effects.

9. Based on physiological changes with age, which of the following sexual dysfunctions is *less* likely among older men than younger men?
   a. premature ejaculation
   b. hypoactive desire disorder
   c. male erectile dysfunction
   d. male orgasmic disorder

10. Which of the following is a recommended content issue in therapy with older adults?
   a. encouraging clients to make new social contacts
   b. helping clients deal directly with fear of death
   c. not attributing personal problems to medical or social problems
   d. keeping up spirits despite difficulties

SHORT ANSWER

1. Are older people more similar or more different than younger people? Explain briefly.

2. Your older friend seems confused. What behaviors might you look for to determine if your friend is experiencing delirium or dementia?

3. Why do we tend to ignore psychological problems in older people?

4. What are common causes of paranoia in the elderly?

5. Briefly describe the issues in medication misuse among the elderly.

6. What is the general approach to treating sexual dysfunctions in the elderly?

7. Identify three general issues in treatment and care of the elderly.

8. Summarize a study suggesting that even good-quality nursing home care may be undesirable.

9. Identify three problems in caring for the elderly in the community.

10. Explain "life review" as an issue in therapy with the elderly.

◆ ANSWERS TO SELF-TEST, CHAPTER 16

MULTIPLE-CHOICE

1. b (p. 458)
2. b (p. 461)
3. c (p. 462)
4. d (p. 468–469)
5. a (p. 470)
6. b (p. 475)
7. d (p. 477)
8. d (p. 480)
9. a (p. 482)
10. b (p. 489)

SHORT ANSWER

1. Despite stereotypes, older people are more diverse than younger. (p. 459)

2. Delirium tends to have rapid onset, not just forgetful but overtly confused thinking and speech, bewildered, sleep-wake cycles disrupted, nightmares and hallucinations more likely. (p. 467–468)

3. We assume problems are due to old age and physical decline. This is not true (or only partly true) in most cases. (p. 470)

4. Results from attempts to fill in gaps in understanding caused by memory or sensory losses, social isolation, etc. (p. 474)

5. Illnesses result in using more drugs while changing metabolism increases risk of side effects. Multiple drugs may interact. Elderly may get confused and take drugs incorrectly. Limited finances lead the elderly to not take drugs as prescribed and to share drugs. (p. 477–478)

6. Treated the same way as for younger people, although with special consideration for physical changes and limits, and remembering that sex was a taboo topic when they grew up. Educate on changes with aging. (p. 483–484)

7. Professionals are less likely to notice, refer problems. They have lower expectations for improvement. This despite the elderly being more thoughtful, thus, seemingly, more amenable to therapy. (p. 484)

8. Elderly people were randomly assigned to three intensities of professional care. Results showed that more professional involvement increased death rates because the professionals pushed institutional placement. (p. 485)

9. Coordinating services among many agencies with various rules. Health care professionals don't enjoy working with problems of elderly. Conflicts with family members who feel angry, guilty, etc. over care issues. (p. 488)

10. Older people often seek, and may benefit from, reviewing their lives and considering the meaning and implications of their lives and experiences. (p. 491)

Chapter 17

Outcomes and Issues in Psychological Intervention

◆ OVERVIEW

The previous chapter completed the text's discussion of major forms of abnormal behavior. Chapter 17 begins the last section of the text, which covers issues in abnormal psychology. These issues underlie many topics covered earlier and round out discussion of the field.

Chapter 17 discusses issues in psychological intervention. Psychological interventions for various disorders were covered in the chapters on those disorders. Chapter 17 brings these interventions together and discusses efforts to integrate them. Chapter 18 deals with legal and ethical issues. Legal issues include insanity, competency to stand trial, and involuntary commitment. Ethical issues concern the rights of research participants and therapy clients.

CHAPTER SUMMARY

Chapter 17 is devoted to evaluating, comparing, and integrating psychological interventions. Many of these approaches to psychological treatment were introduced in earlier chapters.

General Issues in Evaluating Psychotherapy Research discusses the related but different goals of psychotherapy researchers seeking to conduct quality research and psychotherapists seeking to help individuals in the real world.

Review of Psychoanalytic Therapies summarizes therapy approaches growing out of Freud's work. Classical psychoanalysis focuses on repressed childhood conflicts while briefer analytic approaches focus more on current life issues. Evaluations of these approaches have looked at both theoretical issues and research on their effectiveness.

Review of Client-Centered Therapy covers Carl Rogers' approach. Rogers originated the field of psychotherapy research and his model has shown modest effectiveness. *Review of Gestalt Therapy* discusses the similar, but more technique-oriented Gestalt approach which has been less studied.

Review of Behavioral and Cognitive Therapies reviews and evaluates counterconditioning, operant, and cognitive therapies. These approaches, growing out of research traditions, have been more clearly defined and studied in recent years. For example, Ellis' and Beck's cognitive approaches have been extensively studied and compared. Other issues in this area include questions of how to generalize and maintain therapy gains. Generally these approaches have shown considerable effectiveness and raise significant issues for the field.

Review of Couples and Family Therapy and *Review of Community Psychology* reviews these two other approaches to intervention and issues in their use.

Psychotherapy Integration discusses efforts to bring together the various approaches. Wachtel's classic effort to integrate psychoanalysis and behavior therapy illustrates how seemingly disparate approaches to therapy can benefit from each other's ideas. More generally, Lazarus and Messer have debated various ways of integrating therapy approaches and the desirability of doing so.

Cultural and Racial Factors in Psychological Intervention closes the chapter by reemphasizing the need to be aware of cultural differences in therapy with individuals from different backgrounds.

ESSENTIAL CONCEPTS

1. Psychological interventions can be evaluated in terms of both their theoretical assumptions and their empirical effectiveness.

2. Research is essential to evaluate and improve psychotherapy. However, research needs for standardization differ from therapist needs to individualize therapy for each client.

3. Classic psychoanalysis (which seeks to lift childhood repressions) and briefer psychodynamic therapies (focusing more on current life issues) are difficult to evaluate. The nature of "insight" and "therapeutic relationship" raises important, complex issues. Generally, research shows inconsistent to modest benefits.

4. Client-centered therapy assumes that, by valuing clients and understanding their perspective, therapists create conditions in which clients can find their own answers and goals. Psychotherapy research originated in client centered therapy and has shown its benefits generally, although core assumptions of the theory remain unclear.

5. Gestalt therapists have developed many powerful techniques but resist formal evaluation of their effectiveness.

6. Behavioral and cognitive approaches have led to a wide range of therapy techniques.

7. Counterconditioning techniques (based on classical conditioning) have proven effective with a wide range of problems. Operant techniques have also been effective, especially with children.

8. Cognitive therapists propose that actions (and problems) result from the way people make sense out of their world. Cognitive therapists include Ellis and Beck.

9. Ellis seeks to convince clients that their irrational assumptions lead to difficulties. Research supports his approach in some cases, although deciding what assumptions are "irrational" becomes ethically complex. Beck encourages people to examine the evidence for their assumptions and has shown success, although the way in which his methods lead to change is unclear.

10. Cognitive and behavioral therapies have paid special attention to how therapy progress can be generalized and maintained after therapy ends.

11. Cognitive and behavioral therapies are more subtle than is initially obvious. They address many historical issues in psychology and, in practice, utilize a range of approaches to effect change.

12. Couples and family therapists use a wide range of approaches to address communication problems that develop in long-term relationships. They have shown significant results although pragmatic issues remain.

13. Community psychology seeks to prevent problems in populations. Doing so is a challenge and is difficult to evaluate. This approach grew out of, and continues to reflect, the social activism issues of the 1960s.

14. Integration of various interventions remains a challenge. Wachtel has proposed integrating psychoanalysis and behavioral therapies. He emphasizes that current behaviors may both reflect and maintain childhood issues in a cyclical manner and that each theory can benefit from the methods and emphases of the other.

15. Integration of psychotherapy schools can occur in many ways as illustrated by a debate between Lazarus and Messer. Lazarus argued for adopting useful techniques from any theory without adopting the theory. Messer argued that we can only understand and utilize techniques in terms of our theories.

16. Cultural and racial differences can confuse understanding and limit communication between therapist and client.

KEY TERMS

Efficacy (p. 496)

Effectiveness (p. 496)

Therapeutic [working] alliance (p. 500)

Triadic reciprocality (p. 508)

Paradoxical intentions (p. 510)

Multimodal therapy (p. 514)

Technical eclecticism (p. 521)

Common factorism (p. 521)

Theoretical integration (p. 521)

◆ STUDY QUESTIONS

GENERAL ISSUES IN EVALUATING PSYCHOTHERAPY RESEARCH (p. 495–497)

1. Describe four differences between therapy as researched and therapy as practiced and the basis or reason for each. Describe two impacts of managed care and two ways some professionals are responding to it. (p. 495–497)

REVIEW OF PSYCHOANALYTIC THERAPIES (p. 497–501)

2. Describe three basic emphases in classical psychoanalysis and four modifications of it. (p. 497–498)

3. Briefly identify five general issues in the evaluation of classical psychoanalysis. Describe four conclusions of research on classical psychoanalysis. Evaluate brief psychodynamic therapies by summarizing the result of outcome research and four results of process research. (p. 499–501)

REVIEW OF CLIENT-CENTERED THERAPY (p. 501–502)

4. Summarize the basic concepts of client-centered therapy in about five points. Evaluate client-centered therapy in eight points. (p. 501–502)

REVIEW OF GESTALT THERAPY (p. 502–503)

5. Why has little research been done on Gestalt therapy? Summarize the basic concepts of Gestalt therapy in about three points and evaluate it in two points. (p. 502–503)

REVIEW OF BEHAVIORAL AND COGNITIVE THERAPIES (p. 503–515)

6. In general, how do behavioral and cognitive methods approach therapy? Evaluate counterconditioning and exposure methods by describing their approach to therapy and their effectiveness (about two points each). Evaluate operant methods by describing their approach to therapy and their effectiveness (about two points each). (p. 503–504)

7. For Ellis' cognitive (Rational-Emotive) approach describe (a) its goal, (b) its general effectiveness, and (c) why defining irrationality involves an issue of ethics. For Beck's cognitive approach describe (a) its goal in comparison to Ellis, (b) its general effectiveness, and (c) two other issues. Compare these two approaches in three points. Summarize six additional reflections on cognitive behavior therapy. (p. 504–508)

8. What is meant by "generalization and maintenance of treatment effects"? Identify five ways cognitive and behavioral therapists encourage these goals. Summarize the text's views of five basic issues in cognitive and behavior therapy. (p. 508–515)

REVIEW OF COUPLES AND FAMILY THERAPY (p. 515–517)

9. What concept underlies all couples and family therapies? Evaluate these approaches by describing (a) their general effectiveness and (b) predictors of good and poor outcomes. (p. 515–517)

REVIEW OF COMMUNITY PSYCHOLOGY (p. 517–519)

10. What is the basic goal of community psychology? Evaluate this area by identifying three reasons it is difficult to study. Summarize two political factors that contributed to the development of community psychology and two issues in the field currently. (p. 517–519)

PSYCHOTHERAPY INTEGRATION (p. 519–524)

11. Summarize Wachtel's view on integrating psychoanalysis and behavior therapy by describing (a) his principal position and (b) four things behavior therapists can learn from psychoanalysts. (p. 519–521)

12. Identify three general ways in which psychotherapy approaches can be integrated. Summarize Lazarus' and Messer's views on the topic in three points each and Messer's conclusion. Why does the text argue against premature integration? (p. 521–524)

CULTURAL AND RACIAL FACTORS IN PSYCHOLOGICAL INTERVENTION (p. 524–527)

13. Why are cultural and racial factors especially important in psychotherapy? Identify several factors affecting therapy with each of four minority groups. How can recognizing these differences contribute to a more complete science of behavior? (p. 524–527)

◆ SELF-TEST, CHAPTER 17

(* Items not covered in Study Questions.)

MULTIPLE-CHOICE

1. Most therapists describe themselves as
   a. behavioral.
   b. cognitive-behavioral.
   c. dynamic.
   d. eclectic.

2. The advent of managed care has changed what aspect of practice for psychologists?
   a. theoretical orientation
   b. focus upon underlying causes
   c. accountability
   d. efficacy

3. Early in therapy, Tom has found that he enjoys meeting with his therapist. The two seem to be working toward a common goal, and the time appears to go quickly. This would characterize a good
   a. efficacy.
   b. initial symptom reduction.
   c. process.
   d. working alliance.

4. Exposure and counterconditioning methods have been most effective in treating
   a. anxiety.
   b. children.
   c. addictions.
   d. criminals.

* 5. As part of treatment for insomnia, Jack was told to deliberately remain awake. This type of intervention is consistent with a
   a. direct cognitive challenge.
   b. desensitization to the need for sleep.
   c. paradoxical intervention.
   d. token economy.

6. A common element across therapies, regardless of paradigm, is
   a. focusing directly upon symptoms.
   b. challenging irrational beliefs.
   c. determining stimuli that control dysfunctional behavior.
   d. maintaining a positive relationship between therapist and client.

7. The basic goal of community psychology is
   a. affordable treatment.
   b. community-based treatment.
   c. stable communities.
   d. prevention.

8. A problem in rapprochement between different theories of psychotherapy, according to Lazarus,
   a. is that adherents to different theories simply cannot process the necessary information across all paradigms.
   b. is based in large part on empirical findings.
   c. has been based in reluctance to find common factors.
   d. is based on how different approaches define facts.

9. Which of the following are factors that contribute to better outcome in therapy?
   a. similarity of cultural background between client and therapist
   b. same gender for therapist and client
   c. similarity of ethnic background
   d. All of the above are correct.

10. Tim, a Native American child, is in treatment for ADHD. He has moved several times in the past two years. This is likely a sign of
   a. his symptom severity; family members cannot tolerate his outbursts.
   b. instability in his family overall, and his immediate family in particular.
   c. paternal instability; that is, frequent job loss necessitating moving.
   d. normal family functioning within his cultural milieu.

SHORT ANSWER

1. Describe the theoretical view of ego analysts.

2. What are characteristics of healthy people according to Carl Rogers' client-centered therapy?

3. What does the text conclude about the therapist qualities emphasized by Rogers?

4. Why do existential therapists reject scientific evaluation of their approach?

5. In general, how do behavioral and cognitive methods approach therapy?

6. Explain the ethical issue underlying irrationality in Ellis' REBT system.

7. What concept underlies all couples and family therapies?

8. Summarize current issues in the field of community psychology.

9. Summarize Wachtel's principal position on psychoanalysis and behavior therapy.

10. Why does the text argue against premature integration of psychotherapy approaches?

◆ ANSWERS TO SELF-TEST, CHAPTER 17

MULTIPLE-CHOICE

1. d (p. 495)	2. c (p. 497)	3. d (p. 500)	4. a (p. 503)
5. c (p. 510)	6. d (p. 514)	7. d (p. 517)	8. d (p. 522)
9. d (p. 524)	10. d (p. 526)		

SHORT ANSWER

1. Ego analysts emphasize current, conscious ego functions that do not directly depend on id energies. Thus, they see people as more able to control current environment and less pushed by unconscious drives. (p. 498)

2. Rogers says healthy people are aware of their own desires and fears. They recognize and pursue their own goals. That is, they march to the beat of their own drum. (p. 501)

3. Concludes it is useful for clinicians to develop such qualities but research does not prove that simply having them is sufficient to produce change. (p. 502)

4. They consider science dehumanizing, especially when applied to individuals and their unique problems. (p. 502)

5. Approach therapy using the methods, approaches, and results of experimental psychology. (p. 503)

6. Nondistressed people likely also hold beliefs that are, strictly speaking, irrational. Ellis has made an ethical decision about what beliefs are desirable. (p. 505)

7. That conflicts are inevitable when people live together. They are best addressed by involving all the family, focusing on communication. (p. 515–516)

8. The field seeks social change but it is not clear (a) how to do so and (b) how to decide what changes to seek, especially when social or ethical values are involved. (p. 519)

9. That present problematic behavior both reflects and maintains childhood conflicts. That is, childhood conflicts contribute to our present behavior and, in turn, results of our present behavior reconfirm the conflict. (p. 520)

10. We could lose important theoretical distinctions and, thus, treatment options. Distinctions may be issues that need to be studied and, perhaps someday, integrated, not just blurred over. (p. 523–524)

Chapter 18

Legal and Ethical Issues

◆ OVERVIEW

The last section of the text consists of two chapters discussing issues in abnormal psychology. The previous chapter covered issues in psychological intervention. It reviewed approaches to intervention and attempts to integrate them. This, the final chapter of the text, turns to legal and ethical issues in abnormal psychology. In studying this chapter, remember that "issues" do not have easy solutions — or they wouldn't be issues. Especially in working with human beings, there are often no easy answers. Thus it is important to anticipate when issues will exist and to understand the various aspects, implications, and options involved in order to handle them as effectively as possible.

CHAPTER SUMMARY

Psychologists struggle with many legal and ethical issues or dilemmas. Legal issues develop when an individual's mental condition becomes an issue in court. In *Criminal Commitment* cases, issues develop when individuals accused of crimes are found incompetent to stand trial or are acquitted by reason of insanity at the time of the crime. In *Civil Commitment* cases, individuals not accused of crimes may be committed to institutions if they are considered mentally ill and dangerous to themselves or others. Debate continues on whether these legal procedures are fair to the individuals involved and to larger society. Recent court rulings have clarified the legal rights of committed individuals, especially those civilly committed. These include rights to be treated in the least restrictive environment possible, to actually receive treatment, and to refuse treatment in some cases. Debate continues on how to protect individual freedoms while protecting society from disturbed individuals.

Ethical Dilemmas in Therapy and Research covers a very broad area of individual rights. For example, psychologists recognize ethical obligations to obtain the informed consent of others before involving them in research and treatment. Yet research participants may behave differently if they completely understand what is being investigated. Further, disturbed patients, under pressure from family and society, may not be able to choose freely or even to understand the consequences of their decisions. Therapists are also ethically and legally obligated to respect the confidentiality of their patients, yet they may have to break confidentiality if, for example, patients are endangering themselves or others. Other dilemmas arise when therapy clients recover memories of childhood abuse. Such problems are true ethical dilemmas that do not always have easy answers.

ESSENTIAL CONCEPTS

1. Criminal commitment applies to individuals suspected of being mentally ill and of breaking laws while civil commitment procedures apply to individuals suspected of being mentally ill and dangerous.

2. The insanity defense deals with an individual's mental state at the time of a crime. Criteria of insanity continue to evolve and to be controversial.

3. Competency deals with an individual's mental state at the time of trial. It also raises difficult issues.

4. Laws on civil commitment vary but, generally, a person can be committed if they are (a) mentally ill and (b) a danger to themselves or others.

5. There is debate as to how accurately mental health professionals can predict the future dangerousness of a mentally disturbed individual.

6. Legal proceedings have addressed the rights of people committed through criminal and civil proceedings. These include the right to care in the least restrictive alternate setting, the right to treatment (not just minimal custodial care), and the right to refuse especially dangerous or noxious treatments.

7. Deinstitutionalization has been an effort to get committed people out of mental hospitals. Unfortunately, it has led to other problems including homelessness.

8. Psychologists also face difficult ethical dilemmas in dealing with research participants and patients.

9. Regulations have been formulated to protect the rights of subjects in psychological research, such as the concept of informed consent — informing the subject of the risks involved in the research and of their right to freely accept or reject participation in the experiment.

10. The ethical codes of various mental health professions dictate that, with certain exceptions, communications between patient and therapist must be confidential. Privileged communication laws extend this protection into the courts.

11. Therapists face additional ethical dilemmas in determining who is the client whose interests they should serve, what the goals for treatment should be, and what techniques may be justified to achieve those goals.

12. Recently therapists have confronted additional dilemmas with clients who recover memories of abuse. Protecting rights of both the alleged victim and perpetrator is complex.

KEY TERMS

Criminal commitment (p. 530)

Civil commitment (p. 530)

Insanity defense (p. 531)

Irresistible impulse (p. 531)

M'Naghten rule (p. 532)

Outpatient commitment (p. 543)

Advanced directive (p. 552–553)

Informed consent (p. 557)

Confidentiality (p. 557)

Privileged communication (p. 557)

◆ STUDY QUESTIONS

CRIMINAL COMMITMENT (p. 530–539)

1. What legal assumption underlies the insanity defense? Trace the history of the insanity defense using five landmark cases, guidelines, and laws. Describe two recent changes (since 1980). Summarize three general points regarding insanity and mental illness. (p. 530–536)

2. Summarize the case of *Jones v. United States* and the Supreme Court's decision. Explain three additional problems with the concept of legal insanity illustrated by this case. (p. 536–537)

3. Distinguish between “insanity” and “competency.” What is the basic legal principle behind competency to stand trial? Compare the consequences of the two and the issues underlying “synthetic sanity.” Explain the issue of insanity and capital punishment and illustrate its implications. (p. 537–539)

CIVIL COMMITMENT (p. 539–554)

4. Identify the principle underlying civil commitment, common criteria, and common types of commitment procedures. (p. 539–541)

5. How dangerous are former mental patients? Evaluate traditional research on predicting dangerousness and practical criteria that can be used. Describe more recent research on predicting dangerousness and ways to control potentially dangerous former patients. (p. 541–543)

6. Summarize the recent trend in voluntary/involuntary commitments. Why are courts protecting rights of individuals threatened with involuntary commitment? (p. 543–547)

7. Summarize three recent trends protecting the rights of individuals who have been committed. How do ethical free will issues underlie these trends? How do Paul and Lentz propose to deal with these seemingly contradictory rights? (p. 547–553)

8. What factors led to deinstitutionalization policies? What were the unintended results? What future do Gralnick and others fear? (p. 553–554)

ETHICAL DILEMMAS IN THERAPY AND RESEARCH (p. 554–564)

9. Give three examples outside psychology that point to the need for ethical restraints in research. In current research, what process protects participants, and what two recent developments threaten that protection? (p. 554–557)

10. Summarize five ethical dilemmas, being sure to point out why each is a dilemma (i.e., why it is not easily resolved). (p. 557–563) Distinguish, especially, between confidentiality and privileged communication. (p. 557)

11. Summarize the ethical and legal issues involved in reports of recovered memories. Summarize the textbook's concluding comments. (p. 563–564)

◆ SELF-TEST, CHAPTER 18
(* Items not covered in Study Questions.)

MULTIPLE-CHOICE

1. Criminal and civil commitment can be best distinguished by
   a. whether the one being committed is insane.
   b. whether a crime has been committed by the individual.
   c. the severity of the symptoms and the crime committed.
   d. the type of police intervention necessary.

2. The Insanity Defense Reform Act shifted the burden of proof onto the
   a. defense.
   b. prosecution.
   c. expert witness.
   d. judge.

3. In the *Jones v. United States* case, the Supreme Court decided that a person could be considered dangerous
   a. if he or she is in a mental hospital and had previously committed a crime.
   b. only if the prosecutor proved beyond a reasonable doubt that he or she represents a danger to others.
   c. only if he or she had previously committed a violent crime.
   d. if he or she committed a crime that might have led to violence (even if not violent itself).

4. When someone is determined incompetent to stand trial, what typically happens to them?
   a. They are released.
   b. They are treated, then tried for the original crime.
   c. They are treated, then released.
   d. They are treated while serving time in prison for the crime.

5. Monahan suggests that the prediction of violence is most accurate under which of the following conditions?
   a. in nonemergency situations
   b. when the person is currently in the hospital because of past dangerous behavior
   c. in an emergency, when violence appears imminent
   d. when a person can be evaluated over a period of time by a number of professionals in a controlled environment

*6. The *Tarasoff* decision has created concerns over duty to warn in which of the following situations?
   a. Sam, who has indicated to his therapist that he may abuse his children when angry.
   b. Tony, who is HIV-positive, and continues to engage in unprotected sex.
   c. Alison, who has threatened to destroy her ex-boyfriend's car.
   d. All of the above are recent issues that have been considered under the *Tarasoff* decision.

7. "Right to refuse treatment" involves the rights of
   a. patients to refuse hospitalization.
   b. patients to refuse dangerous drugs.
   c. hospitals to refuse to treat dangerous patients.
   d. hospitals to refuse optimal treatment as long as they provide basic care.

8. Deinstitutionalization has been described as an improper label because
   a. most patients end up in treatment in outpatient clinics, thus visiting other institutions.
   b. most deinstitutionalized patients remain mentally ill.
   c. patients typically end up in other long-term care institutions.
   d. few patients are actually discharged from the hospital.

9. Human subjects committees and institutional review boards
   a. have been proposed by the American Psychological Association.
   b. have been outlawed since the Nuremburg war trials.
   c. are used to ensure subjects participate in scientifically significant research.
   d. are used to protect the safety and rights of research subjects.

10. Confidentiality is based on ___________, whereas a privileged communication is ___________.
   a. state law; decided by the individual therapist.
   b. the ethical code of a profession; based on law.
   c. the therapist's obligation not to disclose information; the client's obligation not to disclose opinions about the therapist.
   d. verbal report in therapy; a written report of the therapist's impression of a client.

SHORT ANSWER

1. Summarize the American Law Institute guidelines for defining criminal insanity.

2. Summarize the case of *Jones v. United States*.

3. What issues underlie synthetic sanity?

4. On what basis may individuals be committed to a mental hospital against their will (civil commitment)?

5. How dangerous are former mental patients?

6. Why are courts protecting the rights of individuals threatened with involuntary commitment?

7. What is the ethical issue in "informed consent"?

8. Give several reasons (the text lists four) why therapists may reveal things clients tell them even when state law provides privileged communication for therapy relationships.

9. Describe the ethical issue of "who is the client."

10. What is the ethical issue in reports of recovered memories of child abuse?

◆ ANSWERS TO SELF-TEST, CHAPTER 18

MULTIPLE-CHOICE

1. b (p. 530, 539)
2. a (p. 533)
3. d (p. 536)
4. b (p. 538–539)
5. c (p. 542)
6. d (p. 546)
7. b (p. 550)
8. c (p. 553)
9. d (p. 556)
10. b (p. 557–558)

SHORT ANSWER

1. A person is not responsible for criminal conduct if at the time of such conduct as a result of mental disease or defect he lacks substantial capacity either to appreciate the criminality (wrongfulness) of his conduct or to conform his conduct to the requirements of law. (p. 532)

2. Jones was arrested for a misdemeanor but was found insane. As a result he was hospitalized for longer than he could have been imprisoned if found guilty. Supreme Court ruled it did not matter as he was being treated, not punished. (p. 536)

3. Drugs could be used to make a person synthetically sane to stand trial. But they might not work, produce dangerous side effects, give the jury a false impression, etc. (p. 538–539)

4. If they are mentally ill *and* dangerous to others or themselves (which may include being unable to take care of themselves). (p. 541)

5. Despite stereotypes, research indicates they are, generally, no more dangerous than people in general. Exception is substance abusers, who are more likely to be dangerous (whether ex-patients or not). (p. 541–542)

6. Courts are enforcing the same due process rights that are granted to individuals threatened with loss of freedom for other reasons (such as those accused of crimes). (p. 544–547)

7. People may feel pressured into consenting or may not understand what they're consenting to. Thus their "consent" may be meaningless. (p. 557)

8. (a) Client files suit against therapist, (b) client is being abused, (c) client started therapy to evade law, (d) client is dangerous to self or others. (p. 558)

9. Refers to situations where the therapist has responsibility to several individuals or entities whose interests may differ. Therapist may not be able to serve both interests. (p. 558)

10. Dangers both in encouraging and discouraging clients to recover memories. Encouragement could lead to false diagnosis. Discouragement could mean the memory remains repressed but hampers the client's current life. (p. 563–564)

NOTES

NOTES

NOTES

NOTES

NOTES

NOTES

NOTES

NOTES

NOTES